鎮郡山水總圖
象山
府城
運河
京峴山
丹徒港
大港
北山港
馬蹟山
圌山
黃鶴山
丹陽縣城
九曲河
陵口
柵口
沙

LEAVES OF PRAYER

LEAVES OF PRAYER

The Life and Poetry of He Shuangqing, a Farmwife in Eighteenth-century China (Second Edition)

Selected Translations from Shi Zhenlin's
West Green Random Notes

Elsie Choy

Chinese Calligraphy by
T. C. Lai

The Chinese University Press

Leaves of Prayer
By Elsie Choy

ISBN 962–201–883–1

First edition 1993
Second Edition 2000

Chinese Calligraphy by T. C. Lai

THE CHINESE UNIVERSITY PRESS
The Chinese University of Hong Kong
SHATIN, N. T., HONG KONG
Fax: +852 2603 6692
+852 2603 7355
E-mail: cup@cuhk.edu.hk
Web-site: www.cuhk.edu.hk/cupress

Printed in Hong Kong

Dedicated to the memory of my parents and my sister.

Contents

Listing of He Shuangqing's Poetry

Foreword

This book brings to light the time-obscured poems of a young Chinese woman of the eighteenth century. It not only presents her poems, but it tells the extraordinary story of her life. He Shuangqing (pronounced as Ho Shuang-ch'ing in Wade-Giles romanization), young, beautiful, gifted, was married at the age of eighteen to an illiterate farmer incapable of understanding her. She was treated harshly, and underwent rough physical labor daily; she lived out her brief life under conditions far from favorable to writing poetry.

That it is possible for her poems and the details of her life to be known now, after having been lost sight of for more than two hundred years, is due to the remarkable notebook of Shi Zhenlin, a scholar, and enthusiastic admirer of her work, and to the present translator of his records and her poems. One of those happy coincidences that occur only rarely is that this scholar and poet met. An equally rare event is that his work and hers should be so enthusiastically rendered for today's readers.

Shi Zhenlin's notebook lets us see something of the times. We are given a look, for example, at the interests and modes of life of a group of scholars and poets; we can see into their studios, one of them furnished with a bamboo divan, stone tables, a "cedar root" to sit on, and poems written on the walls. Entries in the notebook indicate the Chinese appreciation of landscape and the nuances of the sun and moon, as shown by the entry, "One evening we went out to enjoy the twilight over the hills." The scholars' aesthetic appreciations were integral to their concepts of "the Way."

It was a happy coincidence for He Shuangqing, in her narrow and restricted milieu, that she should have lived near, and been in communication with, the highly sensitive scholar, Shi Zhenlin, who recognized the value of her poems and who was familiar with the details of her difficult life, which he preserved so vividly in his notebook.

From her youth, He Shuangqing had the urge to write poetry, and along with the gift she had the necessary strength of will to succeed. She needed that strength. Frail, over-worked, she spent the days planting, harvesting, threshing, cooking rice, washing and mending clothes, duties carried on even when she was suffering from malaria. She not only carried out her onerous duties but, according to her chronicler, did so always with a sweet and smiling expression. One can only wonder how she had strength for, or found time for, her writing.

The poet lived in an age and a society not advantageous to women. She fully realized this, and hoped by her writing to improve the attitude of society. She accepted her own place as a "filial daughter-in-law" and carried out her duties with fidelity and grace. She lived up to her high concept of morality, "I treasure myself like a piece of jade," she wrote. She was a Buddhist, and her Buddhist convictions helped to lift her spirit above her material surroundings. That help, plus her indomitable determination to capture and express beauty in her poetry, imbued her with the strength she needed.

He Shuangqing was well aware of her talent. As to her writing, she said, "my poetry simply comes by itself," and she showed her mastery of it in the illustrative line: "The lotus inherits its nature." Her poems, meticulously translated here, sometimes express the vicissitudes and sorrows of her life, and sometimes her joyful and sensitive experience of beauty, especially the beauty of nature.

We share her pleasure in the beauty of some scene through

such delicately wrought lines as, "Moonlight trickles its brilliance ... Splinters the sunset's glow ..." or "fine silk/Tender as rain." Her spirit is stirred by flowers and the moon, by a "lonely goose against the sky." She sees the spring as "a vision dyed light pink." As she cooks her rice, she looks at some chrysanthemums she has planted, thus experiencing activity on two levels at once.

The story of her life provides a vivid example of how mental and spiritual forces can dominate the flat facts of circumstances. Her persistence in writing her poems in spite of so many obstacles, her patience and "sweetness" of attitude show both her spiritual stamina and the beauty of her personality.

He Shuangqing had the rare good fortune, so unlikely in her restricted circumstances, to have her poetry known and admired by a sympathetic and gifted scholar who made her writing and her personality known to other scholar-poets, who, in turn, recounted their amazed admiration. Thus, she had readers who could appreciate the uniqueness of a farmer's-wife-poet enough to write a poem on "a peony leaf." That she had not only the gift to write, but a devotee who kept her work alive, leads us to think that though her life was a hard one, she was, after all, a fortunate person. She would have agreed.

Though Shi Zhenlin made her work known and kept it alive in his lifetime, knowledge of it soon faded. But that is not the end of the story. He Shuangqing has been discovered again, this time by a woman sympathetic to her aesthetic and moral attitudes, and akin to her in poetic sensibility. Elsie Choy's wide knowledge of Chinese history and poetry enables her to understand the background of the period in which the poet wrote, and her translation and notes are solidly based on scholarly research.

In this present work, He Shuangqing's poems are brought back into the light, rich with the glow of true appreciation and lively enthusiasm.

Dorothy Donnelly

Preface

I wish to express my grateful appreciation to the many persons who have encouraged and helped me in this work.

I am indebted to the late Dorothy McGuigan, formerly of The University of Michigan, who happened to befriend me when I was starting my search for He Shuangqing. Being a pioneer on the subject of women, Mrs. McGuigan gave me heart during my long frustrating search; her interest never faltered even when she became seriously ill. My only consolation was that before she went to the hospital for the last time, I was able to bring her the news of my finding He Shuangqing's life and work in their entirety and my discovery of her chronicler, Shi Zhenlin, in his *Xiqing sanji*.

My old friend, Dr. Aileen H. Wei, Professor Emeritus from Seton Hall University, graciously invited me to her home for a week so that we could go over my draft translation of the partial collection of He Shuangqing's poetry I had unearthed at that time. Dr. Wei was my resource person whenever I had questions on the remote meaning of words and phrases in Shi Zhenlin's writing. Professor Wen Hsu of Northwestern University kindly went over that poetry translation to suggest important changes.

I also benefited from friends who read over the manuscript when it was part of a larger project at the beginning. These include Dorothy Donnelly, Eleanor Munro, Cynthia (Toni) King, Mary Arnheim and Dr. Rudolf Arnheim, Professor Emeritus of the Psychology of the Arts from Harvard University. Others were: Professor Julia C. Lin of Ohio University, Professor Emeritus James I.

Crump and Professor Shuenfu Lin, both of The University of Michigan. My thanks to them all for the generosity of their time and counsel, as a result of which I decided to concentrate my efforts on the translation of Shi Zhenlin's writing and He Shuangqing's poetry with some notes and comments of my own, as presented here.

In 1986, two dear young people spent time with me to edit the work. Jean B. Oggins, who became interested in He Shuangqing on our first meeting, offered to edit the prose, while Justin, my son, lent me his ear to fine-tune the poetry translation. During the sweltering heat of that Michigan summer, my dear friend, Dorothy Donnelly, wrote the foreword for me. As a poet herself, Mrs. Donnelly's sensitivity to He Shuangqing's work—indeed, some of Mrs. Donnelly's published lines echo those of the poet's—points to the fact that poetry knows no cultural boundary or time. My gratitude to them in sharing with me this stretch of a long journey. As for mistakes in the translation, naturally I am solely responsible for them.

The manuscript was revised with added notes at the advice of The Chinese University Press. My appreciation for the guidance of their reader and for the help of Jean B. Oggins who again helped in the editing. My son and my daughter, Justin and Puwen, did the final polishing, and my daughter-in-law, Margaret Zhou, lent me a hand with the typing.

The sketch of He Shuangqing was done for me by Professor Liang Hongwen of Qinghua University when she was a visiting scholar at The University of Michigan in 1985. The calligraphy for the original Chinese poetry in "The Poetry" section is done by Mr. T. C. Lai, well-known scholar, author and calligrapher of Hong Kong. My gratitude to them both for their sensitive contribution to the visual presentation.

My appreciation also goes to the Asia Library of The University of Michigan for facilitating my research with one of the top collections of Chinese books in this country and for having the invaluable *Xiqing sanji* by Shi Zhenlin.

Both the City Hall Library and the American Library in Hong Kong extended to me the use of their reference facilities for my proofreading during the late spring of 1989. This, together with an indispensable typewriter lent me by my dear friend, Robert Y. F. Tam, allowed me to finish this phase of work with a thankful heart.

Finally, I would not have been able to spend the countless hours on this work without the devoted support of my husband, who indulgently let me use half of his architectural studio to immerse myself in this labor of love.

Thoughts for the Second Edition

Life comes in cycles, affording us time to reflect on the meaning and mystery of our journey. *Leaves of Prayer* has given me some memorable pauses, which I would like to share with my readers on the eve of its second edition.

A special acknowledgment on my good friend, Author and Critic Eleanor Munro, who wrote the commentary for the book's jacket. Ms. Munro and I have corresponded with each other for over twenty years. She was one of my readers, and she wrote the commentary from her deep empathy with He Shuangqing. It wasn't until 1996 when I was in New York before I was able to call on her and thank her in person for all the encouragement and help she has given me. Her response was simply that writers should be helpful to other writers. We felt we had met each other long before.

In June of 1993 a copy of the newly published *Leaves of Prayers* was brought by Professor Shuenfu Lin, Director then of Chinese Studies at the University of Michigan, to a Yale conference on "Women writers of Ming and Qing." Unknown to him, in a group of four papers he chaired, there turned out to be three on He Shuangqing and/or Shi Zhenlin's *Xiqing sanji*. This was how *Leaves of Prayer* made its debut in the United States.

In a recent interview, I was asked how in my search for the poet I concluded that Shi Zhenlin's records of her were the source of her life and work. I said the integrity in Shi' writing simply speaks for itself. I then cited the following incident as a confirmation after the fact.

In 1989, after delivering the draft of my manuscript to the Chinese University Press in Hong Kong, I came home and picked up Lin Yutang's *Importance of Understanding*. The preface of his book put me into shock. Lin in disbanding his library for travel, wrote that he kept only two books with him afterwards. These were books that he considered nourishing to his soul. They were *Six Chapters of a Floating Life* by Shen Fu and *Xiqing sanji* by Shi Zhenlin, each in its various editions. In his book which is a translation of choice Chinese belle-lettres, he had included four essays from Shi's *Xiqing sanji*. He also announced that one day he would like to write about a farmer's daughter who was a first rate poet. Imagine my frantic search through the book to see if he mentioned that this farmer's daughter is found in Shi Zhenlin's *Sanji*. To my relief he kept that part of the story untold.

The above shows that He Shuangqing was not completely forgotten in modern times. However, I am happy I started my search for her without any previous knowledge of the person. I was free to chart my own course. I had the latitude to explore the historical, social and spiritual elements in the poet's life to arrive at an independent understanding of her as a unique individual with a vision beyond her society's. This probing helped me to achieve a closeness to the poet to tell her story.

As I work on the second edition of *Leaves of Prayer*, two of my best friends who helped me with the first edition, have now passed away — Professor Emeritus Aileen H. Wei of Seton Hall, New Jersey and Poet Dorothy Donnelly of Ann Arbor. Their friendship, generosity and encouragement will be forever remembered.

Some readers have proposed that *Leaves of Prayer* be used as a text to study the whole individual in the Chinese culture by its records of He Shuangqing's life, work and inner reflection. In this second edition, the inclusion of a bibliography and the indexes will be helpful for this purpose. Their compilations were accomplished with the indispensable help of my son Justin Lee in Beijing and my daughter Puwen Lee in Washington, D. C.

E. C.
Ann Arbor, Michigan, U.S.A.
December 1997

Special acknowledgment, January 2000: The printing of the second edition of *Leaves of Prayer* was suspended in 1998 because of the slow economy in Hong Kong then. Now at the dawn of the new millennium, thanks to the subsidy by an anonymous donor, this second edition will take place. My deepest gratitude for the donor's generosity.

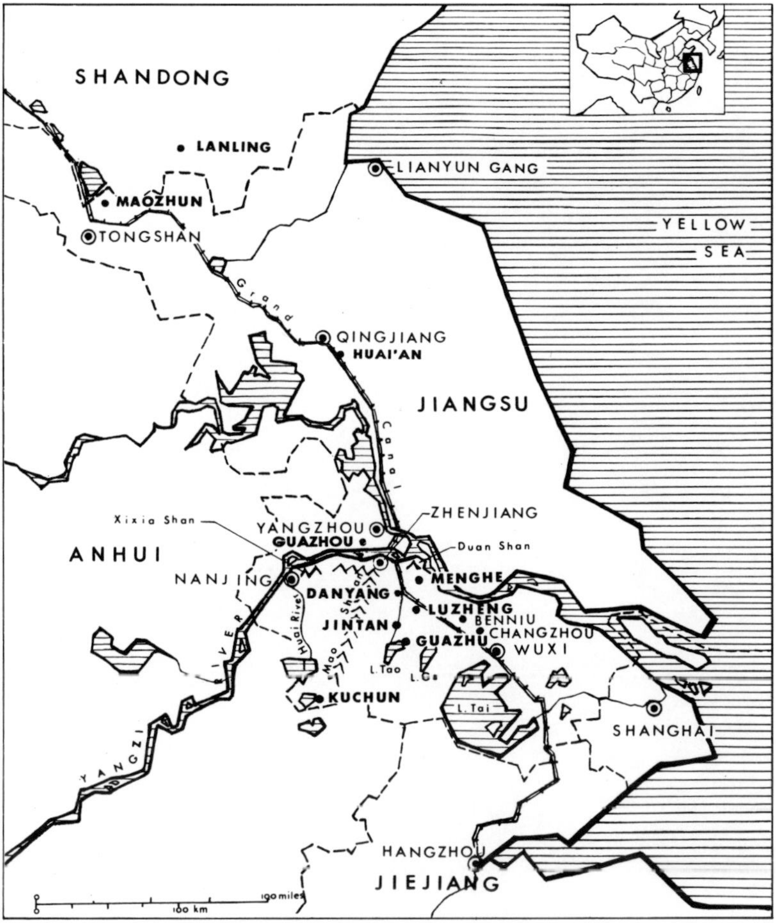

The Lower Yangzi Region

The Poet and Her Chronicler

China owes many of its literary gems to the notebooks of its scholars. These notebooks generally contain an assortment of writings in the form of diary entries, sketches, essays, poetry, letters and random thoughts. Much of this writing is done during moments of reflection, of the author's own volition and without the pressure of an audience, all of which allows for a clear mind and the achievement of full expression of his feelings and spirit. The best pieces from these notebooks are cherished by readers as companions and a constant source of refreshment and inspiration.

One worthy literary notebook, long neglected by the public, is Shi Zhenlin's 史震林 *Xiqing sanji* 西青散記 (West Green Random Notes). It has been neglected because of special circumstances. The publisher of the 1935 edition of the book used for this translation, explains:[1]

> The writing of *Xiqing sanji* is superb. Its records of He Shuangqing 賀雙卿 and her work, as well as the poetry solicited from divination,[2] are especially haunting and beautiful. They have been very popular since their publication in the *Sanji*. ... In recent years people have lifted He Shuangqing's poetry from Shi's book to make up collections under her name; one of these is called *Tianshang renjian* 天上人間 (Heaven on Earth). The result is that Shi Zhenlin's writing has been forgotten.

I think that we might have been steered away from Shi Zhenlin for a purpose. When Shi's *West Green Random Notes* (henceforth called *Xiqing sanji*, or simply *Sanji*) was published in 1738, it enjoyed immediate success on account of the material concerning He Shuangqing.[3] The public admired He Shuangqing as a paragon of virtue; they respected her for her self-education and talent as a poet. Although appalled by her miserable life, they loved her for her compassion and were charmed by her beauty. After Shi's death, editors began to lift her material from Shi's book. Despite their admiration, they viewed as immodest and scandalous her communications with Shi Zhenlin and his scholar friends, and the fact that she had sent her work to Shi for inclusion in his notebook. To circumvent this, they simply censored her story, expurgating this part of her life by obscuring or even removing Shi from the picture altogether.

I was myself a victim of this deception when I started my search for He Shuangqing from my initial acquaintance with her through a Chinese newspaper article published in San Francisco.[4]

At the beginning I had merely the reference cited in the newspaper article to go by. The only copy of that reference in the United States turned out to be in The Library of Congress. From them I obtained a photocopy of a small 72-page volume by He Shuangqing entitled *Xueya xuan ji* 雪壓軒集 (Poetry Collection from the Snow-crushed Studio), edited by Zhang Shoulin 張壽林 and published by the Beijing Cultural Society in 1927. The editor said that the title of this book came from the one cited by Wang Yunshan 王韻珊 in *Guozhao cizhong xubian* 國朝詞綜續編 (Supplement to Qing Poetry), which unfortunately could not be found in the United States.

Zhang's collection of He Shuangqing's poetry consists of fourteen lyric verses and seven regulated poems, occupying twenty pages of the book. The rest of the book deals with references to establish the authenticity of the poet as a person, and an attempt to trace the origin of the title, followed by a compassionate outpouring over the restricted life of Chinese women in general, and the poet's life in particular. Zhang had the highest praise for He Shuangqing's work. He summarized our poet's life as follows:

> He Shuangqing was a beautiful, precocious farmer's daughter born in 1715 at Xiaoshan, Danyang in the lower Yangzi valley (or Jiangnan 江南). Against all odds she became a poet at a time when girls, and especially country girls, were denied an education. From the time she was young, she was enchanted by the written word. It happened that her maternal uncle was the tutor for the neighborhood boys. Shuangqing took the opportunity to listen to their class recitations in an

> adjoining room and committed everything to memory. In this way she educated herself. In her teens she had her uncle exchange her superb needlework for poetry books, through which she learned to write poetry. At eighteen, through matchmaking [presumably], she was married to an illiterate, ill-tempered farmer by the name of Zhou 周 in Jintan. Farmer Zhou and his wilful mother, who was once a wet nurse,[5] were too involved in their struggle for survival to notice the quality of the young bride. They scoffed at her learning; they were only interested in her labor and service as a daughter-in-law. Shuangqing was frail, and having been brought up in the Confucian tradition, was inculcated with a woman's decorum [or the virtue of obedience]. She courageously withstood the poverty, the unremitting toil, the neglect, the assaults and abuse in this uncaring household even when she contracted malaria soon after her marriage. Her husband and mother-in-law ignored her worsening illness, ever demanding a full day's work from her. She did not complain; rather, she served them with a smiling face, masking her grief and depression at all times. In the quiet of the night, however, the welling-up of her heart simply cried for expression; this is the legacy she left us through her poetry which was written on leaves. She died at about twenty-two.

This account conformed with the traditional stories of exemplary virtuous women recorded in injunctions[6] written especially for women before modern times, and for this reason satisfied the general public who did not question it. As a matter of fact, social mores held that a woman should follow the rigid rule of obedience and chastity in the face of hardship or death, for which "trouble" she would be posthumously awarded the honor of having been a "chaste woman" if she remained unmarried after her husband's death; a "brave woman" if she committed suicide to preserve her chastity; or a "brave martyr" if she died or was killed during social or national unrest.

Until recent years, free social intercourse between the sexes was taboo in China. Marriage of two young people was not so much a match between them, as it was between the two families. It was arranged by the parents through a match-maker. Horoscopes were compared and dowry and gifts discussed, but little consultation, if any, was done with the parties involved. As obedience was the first rule toward one's parents, the young people usually accepted the match made for them without protest. They did not see each other until their wedding day. Families of equal social standing were usually matched with one another, but unless it was in a small community, they did not necessarily know each other, and so the agreement to the match by the families depended much on the glibness of the match-maker. Consequently, such marriages sometimes ended in unhappiness. It was not unusual for a woman to be matched to a man many years her senior. In He Shuangqing's case, her husband, Farmer Zhou, was more than ten years her senior. Although she was eighteen by Chinese reckoning, she was actually only seventeen, as the Chinese took the period of a baby's incubation as being one whole year. Reference to the low regard for match-makers can be found in the last translation text entitled "The Daughters of Jin Baiyan."

Parallel to my search for He Shuangqing, I conducted a study on the life of Chinese women through the ages in order to understand the social proprieties expected of them during the eighteenth century. Patriarchy with its clan system and hereditary rule had been established since antiquity. It was taken for granted by the third millennium B.C., long before Confucius (551–479 B.C.) taught it as a system of morality for government and society. Although chastity applied to both men and women at the beginning, the emphasis began to shift during the Han 漢 dynasty (206 B.C.–A.D. 220), when the intelligentsia, drawn mostly from the Confucians, came to fill the bureaucracy, and when Confucianism itself was adopted as the philosophy of government. In 30 B.C., Liu Xiang 劉向 wrote the first injunction for women entitled *Lienu zhuan* 列女傳 (Biographies of Brave Women)[7] as a subtle remonstration to Emperor Cheng (成帝) to guard against the families of his consorts from infiltrating the affairs of the state. Whereas the ancient kings took upon themselves the responsibility for calamities faced by the nation, the latter-day emperors regarded themselves as irreproachable, and, in time of emergency, shifted the blame by demanding greater loyalty from their men. The men, in turn, demanded greater chastity from their women by tightening their restrictions on them. Since one of the "virtues" instilled in women was to obey and to accept their lot without protest, in time, the responsibility of upholding society's morality became placed entirely on them.

This is the basis of Lu Xun's 魯迅[8] denunciation of the later Confucians, and in particular, the Neo-Confucians of the Song 宋 dynasty (960–1279), who regarded themselves as the champions and arbitors of morality. In his 1918 essay, "My Views on Chastity,"[9] Lu Xun pointed out that it was they who pronounced that it was only proper that when a woman's husband died she should remain single or die, and if she was confronted by a ravisher she should also die. He concluded by raising the question, "Have polygamous men the right to praise chastity in women?"

From the Song dynasty onward society's sanctions against women became more and more stringent so that by the Qing 清 dynasty (1644–1911) suicide became the common practice, not only among women whose husbands died, but also among those whose fiancés died. Should a married woman find her marriage intolerable, outside of joining a nunnery, an act that was seldom approved by the families involved, her only alternative was to commit suicide. Statistically this record was supported by a historical survey[10] undertaken in 1971 which shows the number of "brave women" (or those who committed suicide) doubled during the Song dynasty compared to the previous two thousand years of Chinese history, and continuing to climb thereafter so that, by extrapolation, the women's suicide rate in the Qing dynasty ranked the highest in Chinese history.

This was the social milieu in which He Shuangqing lived a model life of chastity, while facing great difficulties in her marriage. If she had committed suicide in accordance with the provisions of the time as was suggested to her by a farm woman friend, she would have been honored as a "brave woman." The fact was that she refused to do so, giving as her reason that according to her Buddhist faith, she had to pay the debts incurred in her previous life. The modern editor Zhang Shoulin, maintained this to be He Shuangqing's reason for living out her short life. We, however, need to examine her life closely before we can accept this as He Shuangqing's true motive.

Two other questions confronted me. First, if He Shuangqing's poetry was written on leaves, how were her twenty-one poems in Zhang's collection collected and handed down? Second, Zhang pointed out that the poet was not "the usual type of conventional shy young lady," yet his story of her life was filled with conventions. Was it the poet or the later editor who was conventional?

However, since I was just so happy to have found what I thought was the complete collection of He Shuangqing's poetry after the long search, I pushed these questions to the back of my mind and started to work on the translation of her poetry.

The literary rendition of her work went smoothly enough; besides, I was fascinated by her images and her felicity in expressing them. But soon I began to find technical discrepancies along the way. Names cropped up here and there in her poetry with no references to her life as told by Zhang. Then, looking for a map of the eighteenth-century Jiangnan or the Classical South along the Yangzi River in which she lived, I consulted the local records[11] of the counties in that area only to find two separate records for Danyang 丹陽 and for Jintan 金壇, which Editor Zhang had said to be the same place. They are actually towns or counties 40 *li* (14.4 miles) apart in the western region of the area. Danyang is located on the Grand Canal (運河) after it crosses the Yangzi River just north of the river at Zhenjiang 鎮江, the metropolitan river port that links north and south China. Jintan, on the other hand, is on a waterway connected to the Canal. Later on I did find an old chorography[12] (or a description and map of an area) that recorded Danyang and Jintan, together with Dantu 丹徒 (or present-day Zhenjiang), as being under the administration of Piling 毗陵 during the fourth century. Since our poet lived in the eighteenth century, Editor Zhang's carelessness in this matter troubled me.

The county records of Danyang[13] where He Shuangqing was born, and of Jintan,[14] where she lived after her marriage, both honored her, but with different emphases. The former did her the honor of listing her as a hometown author under the heading "Literature" with this entry: "He Shuangqing, also named Qiubi 秋碧: *Xueya xuan ji* 雪壓軒集, born at Jiangshu 蔣墅, Danyang and married to the son of a Zhou family in Xiaoshan 綃山, Jintan."[15] Jintan's county records, however, simply recorded her self-education without mention of her as a poet and then put the emphasis on her being a filial daughter-in-law who was obedient to her husband and his mother.[16]

I was not able to find collections of poetry under He Shuangqing's name other than Zhang Shoulin's edition of her *Xueya xuan ji* in the United States. My research did not pick up momentum until I looked into poetry anthologies of Chinese women. I found that He Shuangqing is far from being forgotten in modern times. With but a short lull during the war years from 1933 through the fifties in China, she was represented in an anthology published in 1918[17] and three others from 1926 to 1932,[18] then she appeared again in the years of 1961, 1970 and 1978.[19] The locale of the publication of her work moved from mainland China to Hong Kong and Taiwan after that, and it may be recalled that the impetus for the present search for her life and work came from a Chinese newspaper published in 1978 in the United States. This widening audience and revival of her work suggest a growing interest in her and a recognition of the quality of her poetry. Finally in 1973, or 258 years after her birth, she was named one of the three major women lyric poets in the Qing dynasty by Han Shiqiu 韓石秋 in his *Qingdai wenxue shi* 清代文學史 (History of the Literature of the Qing Dynasty)[20] published in Taiwan. Thus, her importance in Chinese literature was finally recognized.

These sources containing He Shuangqing's work were all sympathetic to her; they told the same story that Zhang Shoulin had told. The only exception was *Nu zuojia shici xuan* 女作家詩詞選 (Selections of Poetry by Women Writers) edited by Tong Renlan 童紉蘭 and Sun Peicai 孫佩茝, published in 1961. In the preface of their book, these authors cited some of He Shuangqing's lines[21] from her "Nine Poems Harmonizing[22] Bailuo" as samples of what they termed "women's hypocritical writing resulting from a sense of womanly propriety imposed on them by Chinese tradition" (details on this will be found on pp. 23–24). On the other hand, they also quoted other lines[23] from the same poem to illustrate genuine and soulful qualities in women's poetry. However, what really caught my attention was their derisive mention of He Shuangqing having communicated with some "so-called scholars."[24]

With this finding, a new He Shuangqing began to emerge from behind Zhang's restricted picture of her as being just an exemplary filial daughter-in-law. This discovery was supported by a modern historian, Wang Fanting 王藩庭, in his *Zhongguo lidai funu* 中國歷代婦女 (Women in Chinese History) published in 1966. The four pages on He Shuangqing's life and work in his book helped fill the gaps left in my initial translation of her poetry.[25] For example, the name of "Bailuo" 白羅 in the poem "Nine Poems Harmonizing Bailuo" referred to the immortal Bailuo whom a scholar by the name of Shi Gongdu 史公度 and his friends had befriended through divination; "Ningxi" 寧溪 in the poem "After Ningxi's Rhyme" turned out to be one of the scholars in this group; and "Mengzhan" 夢覘 of "Harmonizing Mengzhan" was no other than the scholar landlord from whom the Zhou family rented their hut and land in Xiaoshan, Jintan. In addition, these pages clarified an obscure quotation of He Shuangqing's that had been cited by Zhang: "Anshu 闇叔 is sick, Yuhan 玉函 is poor, and I am both. On top of that, I am a woman. How sad! It would be indeed a blessing if I could become a colorful cloud and float away!" This passage now made sense, for Anshu and Yuhan were two of the scholars in the landlord's coterie.

This turn in events prompted me to re-examine Zhang Shoulin's references, which had discouraged me when I first tried to look them up. Of the five references found in his edition of He Shuangqing's *Xueya xuan ji*, two[26] concerning the origin of the title used could not be found because of their obscurity; the third[27] turned out to be wrongly attributed, and the fourth[28] contained a fabricated story of our poet who was given a different name. Much ado was made of these four inconsequential references by Zhang. This, together with his intense lament over the poet's life, reduced the significance of the fifth, or last and most important reference, Shi Zhenlin's *Xiqing sanji*.

Zhang uses evasive tactics to discredit Shi Zhenlin. On page 25 of *Xueya xuan ji*, he acknowledged that He Shuangqing's poetry is to be found in the *Sanji*, but on page 42, he says, "Although the *Sanji* is beautifully written and makes for enjoyable reading, the references on He Shuangqing are scattered in that book and are difficult to ferret out. Recently, however, Bai Yang has taken the references on He Shuangqing from the *Sanji* and made them into a book called *Qianchou ji* 欠愁集 (Collection of Debts Owed). From her book we learn much about He Shuangqing." Again on page 54, he writes, "He Shuangqing did not wish to hand down any of her writing. For this reason, much of her lyrics were lost as soon as she wrote them. Fortunately, a small portion of them can be found in the *Sanji*."

By that time I was beginning to sense that Shi Zhenlin and Shi Gongdu might well be the same person, and so I combed the Asia

Library at the University of Michigan again. I finally located the volume of Shi Zhenlin's *Xiqing sanji*, which is used for this translation, under a series entitled *Zhongguo wenxue zhenben congshu* 中國文學珍本叢書 (Collections of Rare Manuscripts from Chinese Literature).

A cursory look through Shi's book told me at once that I had at last found the complete record on, and source of, He Shuangqing's life and work, with the added delight of her chronicler's sensibilities and superb writing. Before I found this, I had wondered why most of the references that touched on He Shuangqing's life always used the same language, word for word. Now I could see that Shi Zhenlin was the original writer, whose writing simply became the best way of telling our poet's story. Since Shi Zhenlin had recorded four more of He Shuangqing's poems[29] than Zhang Shoulin had, aside from some fragmentary lines that he alone was privileged to obtain, I guessed that he was shunted to the background soon after his death. Thereafter, collections of He Shuangqing's poetry under her name began to appear one after another, and they, in turn, became sources of new editions under her name in the same way that He Shuangqing's *Xueya xuan ji*, as edited by Zhang Shoulin, came into being. The other two collections under her name known at present are: *Tianshang renjian* (Heaven on Earth), as mentioned by Zhang Jinglu in the epilogue of Shi Zhenlin's *Xiqing sanji* published in 1935, and *Qianchou ji* (Collection of Debts Owed) by Bai Yang, a contemporary of Zhang Shoulin, as reported by the latter. The result is that He Shuangqing's poetry collection became an entity separate from Shi Zhenlin's *Xiqing sanji*, and, before long, no one could remember its source. That is why *County Records of Danyang* attributed He Shuangqing as the author of *Xueya xuan ji* with no reference to Shi's *Sanji*. As for Shi Zhenlin, *County Records of Jintan* listed him as one of their honored sons who had passed the imperial examination; it gave a brief summary of his life and works under "Literature"; but it recorded *Xiqing sanji* incorrectly under the heading of "Novelists" where it noted the author's name but said nothing of the book's content.[30]

So much for the long journey toward recovering He Shuangqing's records in the writings of Shi Zhenlin. At this point a few words are needed to explain the acquisition of names by an individual, especially the scholar, in China. It will become quickly apparent that most of Shi's friends in this *Sanji* translation have more than one name. Much emphasis is put on the appropriate name. After receiving a given name from one's family at birth, one may, as one grows older, choose to acquire other names, each reflecting a mode or change in one's life as it develops. Since Chinese names are often custom made, this allows great freedom in forming new personal names to mark significant occasions or a new stage in one's life. This is one area where individuality is respected. There are no fixed rules as to how many names one can acquire or use. The individual may even choose to retire a given name, which generally is reserved for use by the family. Our poet used her given name of Shuangqing in all her writings and this is used by Shi Zhenlin in his *Xiqing sanji*, without any reference to her second name of Qiubi 秋碧 that was reported by Zhang Shoulin and the county records of Danyang and Jintan. In Shi's case, aside from his given name of Gongdu 公度, he used the name Zhenlin 震林 in all his writings and with his friends. In 1723 at the age of thirty, he was addressed by an immortal who responded to a divination session,[31] as "Nongyue Xianlang" 弄月仙郎 (or The Young Immortal Who Plays with the Moon). Shi liked to use this Daoist name when he was in his wandering mood (see translation on p. 80). In addition, another name was chosen for him by a revered friend in 1725 when he was thirty-two, "Wugang" 梧岡.[32] Four years later he changed the first character of this name from one meaning "wutung tree" and therefore, "upright" to "wu" 悟 meaning "enlightenment."[33] The two characters being homonyms, this left the pronunciation intact, but the new character chosen by Shi himself clearly pointed to the ideal which he embraced as he matured.

The lower Yangzi valley where He Shuangqing and Shi Zhenlin lived, covers the alluvial plain where the Yangzi River flows toward, and empties into, the East China Sea north of the city of Shanghai. It extends inland to Nanjing 南京 (or Southern capital), which has served as the seat of government many times in Chinese history. This valley was first settled by two Zhou princes[34] before 1122 B.C. Subsequently the ancient kingdoms[35] that flourished here played roles in Chinese chronicles until this territory was absorbed by Emperor Qin Shihuang 秦始皇 , the first unifier of China in 221 B.C. Aided by the Grand Canal that was built in the Sui 隋 dynasty (A.D. 605–618), this valley became a grain producing and exporting center from the Tang 唐 dynasty (618–905) on. It acquired political prominence in the twelfth century when the Song court abandoned northern China to the Jin 金 invaders and moved southward across the Yangzi River to become what is known as the Southern Song. Following the court, a great number of literati and artisans moved southward and helped to effect a renaissance of Chinese culture that continued to flower after Southern Song's collapse. The capital of the Southern Song was Hangzhou 杭州 (or Kinsai, as the succeeding Mongols called it, and thus the name used by Marco Polo when he described it in superlative terms in *The Travels of Marco Polo*).[36] Three centuries later when the Manchus conquered China forming the Qing dynasty, many of the intellectuals in this area put up an unspoken resistance against the carrot-and-stick policy of Qing that was used to soften their Han loyalty. Some of them, like Shi Zhenlin, retired as soon as they could after a stint in government service, while others refused to serve altogether and became hermits.

This area was to the advantage of these intellectuals, for this valley with its temperate climate, fertile soil and ample rain, afforded a comparatively easy living. It is also in this valley that the

Grand Canal, flowing north and south, crosses the Yangzi River just north of Danyang and Jintan. The Grand Canal, which in the eighteenth century was navigable from Hangzhou all the way to the capital Beijing 北京 , and the Yangzi River, which reaches into the inner heartland of China, have been important thoroughfares through centuries of war and peace in China. Consequently, there was a continuous ferment of ideas among the intelligentsia living in this valley, even though the peasants remained conservative. Furthermore, the distinct seasons and the varied scenery stimulated poets and artists. The gentle landscape with its close network of waterways connecting many lakes, the lush vegetation, and moist climate, produced a perpetual mistiness in the atmosphere, which shrouded both the lower eastern plain and the western mountain peaks and nurtured the imagination of the inhabitants.

As a matter of fact, this misty atmosphere has long led the inhabitants to conjure up images of what might lurk behind the valley's vapor and clouds. This is evidenced in their traditional acceptance of ghosts and spirits, who are believed to be the dead who have gone to dwell in another realm while retaining their earthly sensibilities. Forms of divination have been devised to communicate with these spirits. These folk beliefs were part of the background shared by Shi Zhenlin and his scholar friends. Even though their Confucian teachers ignored a belief in spirits, these young scholars, less orthodox, thought of themselves as free souls and believed "that outside of the classics, there are many things bestowed on men by the gods" (see translation on p. 65). On certain occasions when they became bored by their rigorous studies or needed inspiration, they engaged in divination as a diversion and a method of communication with a different world. Thus, in the early part of his *Sanji*, Shi Zhenlin records many sessions of divination in which he and his friends invited spirits or immortals, most of whom happened to be literate females, soliciting from them their stories told in haunting poetry. The moodiness of this poetry reinforced a general melancholy which came from the scholars' sensitivity toward life, and which influenced their sympathy toward women in particular.

Some of the poetry recorded from the scholars' divination circulated in Jintan. In He Shuangqing's "Nine Poems Harmonizing Bailuo," Bailuo was one of these immortals whose poetry had been recorded through divination. What is very interesting is that once He Shuangqing came to be part of the scholars' circle, she displaced all the immortals conjured by the scholars. It is as if the early records of divination in the *Sanji* anticipated the appearance of He Shuangqing, with the narrator in the person of Shi Zhenlin himself becoming her friend and chronicler. In this way, Shi and his friends were witness to He Shuangqing's short life, the lightning swiftness of which demonstrated for them the precariousness of human existence. Furthermore, as the one who recorded He Shuangqing's work and, as kin to Landlord Mengzhan who hosted his scholar friends, Shi Zhenlin made it possible for his resounding affirmation of her life and poetry to reach his friends and draw them from their former preoccupation with the spirit world. For them she became the personification of the joy and sadness they felt in their own lives.

In 1762, twenty-four years after the publication of *Xiqing sanji*, Shi Zhenlin wrote about it in retrospect in his second notebook, *Huayang sangao* 華陽散稿 (Huayang Essays):[37]

> The four chapters of my *Xiqing sanji* are devoid of emotions but filled with regrets; they can also be said to be devoid of regrets yet filled with emotions. The dreams involving the female characters may be said to be full of shadows but devoid of perfume, yet they are also filled with perfume but devoid of shadows.

Little did he suspect, even at that time, that his encounters with the characters, both male and female, recorded in his book were important experiences for his journey toward maturity and spirituality.

Shi Zhenlin lived from 1693 to 1781 during the Qing dynasty. A native of Guazhu 瓜渚 on Lake Tao 洮, Jintan County, Jiangsu Province, he passed the imperial examination in 1736 and remained in the capital for two years but decided against accepting an appointment in another province in favor of the post of County Professor[38] at Huai'an 淮安, north on the Grand Canal so that he would be nearer to his aged and widowed mother living with his family at home.[39] He served in this capacity until his mother's death five years later, when he retired completely to pursue his poetic vision of life. He spent his remaining years roaming the mountains and streams in the Yangzi valley, keeping company with like-minded individuals whether they were Buddhist monks, Daoist priests, scholars or ordinary folk. He was sought after as a writer, poet, calligrapher and painter, as well as a teacher of these arts, until his death at eighty-eight.

Besides a collection of poetry, *Youxian shicao* 遊仙詩草 (Poetry from an Itinerant Immortal), Shi left us the two literary notebooks, *Xiqing sanji* and *Huayang sangao*. The former traces his development from his twenty-ninth to forty-third year when he was in the north taking the imperial examination (1722–1736), while the latter records his post-*jinshi*[40] days when he became a poet-writer at large.

Shi Zhenlin was sensitive and compassionate in nature. In his 1737 preface for his *Xiqing sanji* published a year later, he introduced himself in this way:

> When I was young, I feared the sudden brightening and darkening of the sky and was told that it was day and night. I could not understand the sudden appearance and disappearance of people and was told that it was birth and death. I was taught the difference between the Big Dipper and Little Dipper, the animals and the fowl. This was the beginning of knowledge for me.
>
> As I grew older, I no longer wondered about the sudden brightening and darkening of the sky and the appearance and disappearance of

> people; I gradually accepted these as normal happenings. However, at times, in reverie, my spirit would soar to the higher realm. I would look down from that height and reflect that within the sudden brightening and darkening of the sky and the appearance and disappearance of people there remains a feeling of sadness.
>
> In infancy I was fed the meat of a hen. My family told me that the hen's babies were still around. I crawled over to the chicks who eyed me with suspicion, while guarding their mother's feathers. I became sad and refused to eat the hen's meat. That was the beginning of sadness for me.

Shi's sensibilities, his respect for life, and his high-mindedness produced a quiet, romantic figure who enjoyed the simple joys of life and lived truthfully to cultivate his poetic vision. In *Xiqing sanji* he guides us through his own milieu, that of the literate class in the lower Yangzi valley, sharing with us the lives of his friends whose sense of values led them to strive for a meaningful life outside of the material world and to cultivate their humanity, even when they faced a life of poverty. With composure he paints for us these scholars at their creative best, without sparing us their foibles, including his own. As a result, we come away from his book finding our sense of humanity confirmed by a soul-searching journey with these enlightened friends through their trials, joys, sorrows, ecstasies and agonies, all of which they openly shared with one another just as Shi does with us.

Being a record of fourteen years during Shi's life, the contents and the moods of this book are varied, but the quality of writing never falters. For instance, an ordinary episode in his recollection of picking cotton, both when he was a child and later with his young son, moves us with poetic pastoral beauty that reveals the adroit naturalness of a master craftsman who wrote with his heart (see translation on pp. 65–66). The same gentle sensibilities are felt in his writing on He Shuangqing.

He Shuangqing was Shi's most engaging and yet most challenging subject. Her tragic life under her ill-fated marriage was made more apparent, rather than diminished, by her adherence to decorum. She was unique in her self-education. It gave her the means and motivation to transcend her suffering by transforming her daily trials into poetry. Shi transcribed her poems as he received them from her. She wrote using pollen or thin ink and he patiently deciphered her small writing on the fragile leaves, acting all the time as a big brother or confidant, listening to, and sharing, the inner thoughts of a young woman caught in the net of tragedy.

Although *Xiqing sanji* was Shi Zhenlin's personal notebook, there was general interest in it among his friends. Shi brought the manuscript with him on his travels and shared it with old friends and new acquaintances. Occasionally his friends contributed material that they felt was worthy. As for He Shuangqing, she was fully aware that as much as she could share her poetry through his book, she also needed some contact with like-minded individuals outside a home that frowned on literacy. Yet, in sending her work to Shi for inclusion in his notebook, she was not counting on leaving her name to posterity as much as she was hoping that her poetry might be helpful to other young women in predicaments similar to her own. She felt that in this way she would not have lived in vain (see translation on p. 90).

Shi Zhenlin does not explain how it was that he made He Shuangqing's acquaintance. Presumably He Shuangqing's scholar landlord, Zhang Mengzhan 張夢覘 , was instrumental in arranging their meeting, since he knew of Shuangqing's talent and since Shi was his cousin. At least it was Zhang's bondmaid who brought the poet's work to Shi Zhenlin every time Shi visited the Zhang brothers in Jintan.

In He Shuangqing, Shi Zhenlin and his friends found a fellow poet restricted in life, yet larger than life in her capacity for understanding and compassion. They were constantly surprised to see her turning her difficult life into memorable lines. They marveled at the ease with which she envisioned her images everywhere she looked, be it the moonlight or the sunset, the field or the pond, in the woodshed or her kitchen. They were touched by her sensitivity in capturing transient beauty within moments of its perception. Above all, they admired her for being true to herself and her rural background. For the tapestry of her work represents no less than her whole being and its relation to nature; it is the fruit of her mind, heart and spirit illumined by the dew she gathered under moonbeams. All this, by the way, is what set He Shuangqing and her work apart from her sister poets, whose vision was unfortunately crippled by their confinement in the inner chamber[41] that was empty of nature's handiwork.

He Shuangqing's use of perishable leaves and flower pollen for writing her poetry has been interpreted as reflecting a pessimistic view of life on her part. The use of leaves by poets is not without precedent in China, just as He Shuangqing herself was known in her teens to have used a cassia leaf to write the whole of the *Xin jing* 心經 .[42] However, where other instances involving the use of red leaves for poetry usually had a romantic overtone,[43] He Shuangqing's dependence on leaves and pollen from flowers as her chief media transcended romanticism. Her use of these media suggests that she was an unconventional person, creative, resourceful, practical, aesthetic and philosophic at the same time. In her husband's home she was not free to read and write, nor could she find time to earn pin money as she had been able to do in her own family. Yet, as she told a neighbor, "With all the emotions constantly welling up in me, my poetry simply comes by itself." Therefore, it was a natural thing for her to use the leaves and flower pollen from the many flowering shrubs that she loved so well in the foothills around her farm house. These were nature's answer to her prayer, an answer that might seem odd to others, but one that well suited her outlook on life. After all, what better way was there for her to achieve an idealistic and transcendent union with the universe than to allow her work, which represented her heart and soul written on fragile leaves, to hasten an early return to the substratum of existence that is believed to be the void out of which all things ceaselessly arise and into which they endlessly return?

We should also consider the fact that Buddhist sutras were at one time written on palm leaves or *Borrassus flabellifor,* which rendered in Chinese is *beiduo* 貝多 , thus making *beiwen* 貝文 the equivalent to Buddhist scripts. As a Buddhist learned in its sutras, He Shuangqing could easily borrow this concept for her own use. Still, for a young person to be so bold and unconventional as to use the very medium for sacred sutras as her own tool, speaks of a confidence that is beyond the ordinary. Her further adoption of flower pollen for writing points to a pre-meditated choice or conviction on her part.

Behind this was He Shuangqing's love of nature, the primary flow of the universe to which humanity adjusted in agrarian China. With her own scholarship extending beyond the Confucian canons taught by her uncle, she had made the literature of Daoism and the sutras of Buddhism a part of her life. The Daoist view of nature as being impartial in its giving and taking was confirmed by her own farm life experience; it also generated a transcendent outlook in her. In time this outlook was illuminated for her by her Buddhist faith, whose *Lengyan jing* 楞嚴經 she quoted in her lines: "Whether sad or bitter, / Life, death are both sweet." (See "Plum Blossoms" written to the tune of *Chun cong tianshang lai* in translation on pp. 127–28.) From this, we know that she was prepared to face both life and death with equanimity.

This philosophic outlook enabled her to see through the confines of her sordid home life and to reach out for the beauty in the greater nature beyond her door. It equipped her with wings to soar into splendor in her own space. Therefore, even though she labored in the day, she was able to drink from the mist hovering over the surrounding peaks; to surrender her heart to the plum blossoms in the spring chill and to the chrysanthemum in the autumn frost; to follow the orioles and the wild geese into the distant blue; to touch the texture of sunset's after-glow; to invite the moonlight into her chamber through her small window; and to pluck the stars from the night sky. In the quiet of the night she offered this harvest to her muse through poetry, and so found sanctuary and repose to sooth the pain and wounds of the day.

While moving toward the attainment of this outlook, she was sped on her path by the deterioration of her home life. Within the first year of her marriage, a series of crises found her coming to the door of enlightenment. This was recorded by Shi Zhenlin in the following manner (see translation on pp. 85–86).

> Shuangqing, though frail physically, maintains a good temper. She is very patient. Even when depressed, she shows herself to be calm and cheerful. When a sympathetic woman visitor in Shuangqing's room scolded and cursed Shuangqing's family about the way they treated her at home, Shuangqing pleaded with the woman to stop. The woman finally said, "Are you a dead toad? How can you be so cowardly?"
>
> One day Shuangqing happened to pause for breath while she was pounding rice. Her husband immediately suspected her of loafing. He shoved her with force and, as she fell on the mortar, the pestle hit her waist. She endured the pain, got up and resumed pounding. Her husband glared at her angrily. She smiled to apologize, saying, "The grain should be ready for threshing now."
>
> For lunch she made rice porridge and was half-way through when she had a flare-up of her malaria. The fire was too strong and so the porridge boiled over. She quickly added some water to the porridge. But her mother-in-law was already upon her, scolding and pulling her by her ear. She yanked at Shuangqing with such force that she tore off Shuangqing's earring, splitting her ear lobe. Shuangqing put a hand over her wounded ear and wept. With the ladle raised, the old woman

threatened her, "How dare you cry!" Shuangqing had to wipe the pot and finish the cooking.

Her husband thought she had overstepped herself and so forbade her to eat lunch that day. Shuangqing continued pounding rice. A neighbor woman asked her, "Aren't you hungry?" She said, "No." The neighbor said, "You feel full because of the rage in you." Shuangqing scooped out the flour from the mortar, then touching the ground with her head [reverently] answered, "May Heaven let me bear all the suffering for all the ill-fated young women in the world so that none of them should ever have a fate like mine!"

Therefore, she asked the servant boy Ling to copy my *Sanji* for her so that when she died, it will be buried with her. She wrote "Nine Poems Harmonizing Bailuo" with rouge on a handkerchief. When Mengzhan asked to see the poems, she declined saying, "You will not understand this, but if I were destined to be another ill-fated beauty in my next life, I would want to be another Shuangqing!" I was given the chance to copy her poems, after which I hastened to return her handkerchief. On it I detected some water spots, which no doubt were tear stains. [italics added]

Significantly, Shi Zhenlin sensed this to be the moment of Shuangqing's enlightenment. Her open request for a copy of his *Sanji* for her burial shows a resolve that was to determine for her the way she wanted to live out the rest of her short life. Her "Nine Poems Harmonizing Bailuo," written at this juncture, holds the key to our understanding of her sudden enlightenment, contrary to what the modern anthologists, Tong Renlan and Sun Peicai, who believe they show only Shuangqing's hypocrisy. The lines in these poems of which they disapprove are:

From Poem II:

Since I can preserve the padded jacket
To keep my husband warm,
My heart is like honey,
I don't reject him.

From Poem III:

The sudden chill in the night
Is accompanied by a fierce wind—
Don't blow at my husband,
Concentrate on me.

We may also add these lines from Poem VII:

When he returns I shall plead
With him to sleep late;
Even when the sun is up,
I will not let anyone disturb him.

Just as He Shuangqing's woman friend berated her for not standing up for her own rights against the family's ill treatment, these modern anthologists have failed to understand the transcendence shown in our poet's lines. In these poems He Shuangqing had taken the significant step on her new path of enlightenment, far beyond worldly ways of humanly calculated right and wrong. Specifically, the lines in question actually express the joy of being an unresentful forgiver; for this reason they are crucial to our understanding of her transcendence. If they were written by her at the beginning of her marriage, they may have conveyed no more than the happiness of a bride. Since they were written after a series of traumatic crises in her life, they signify a level of transcendence that lifted her above the squalor of her home life. It should be noted that she started this poem with: "Since I can't fulfil my vow / Of retiring to a nunnery, / My frozen heart is impassive / Like a still pool." This tells us that she had leaped out of the arena of worldly contention. This transcendence liberated her from the bondage of resentment and enveloped her with a healing blessedness so overwhelming that its compassion overflowed to include both friends and tormentors. That these poems were an important turning point in our poet's life is further indicated by the symbolic red [like blood] of the rouge she used for their writing.

Her ability to rise above the dismal circumstances of her life confirmed for He Shuangqing her self-worth as an individual. Although she was fully aware that her society valued a man's existence over a woman's, she now wished to be no other than Shuangqing herself, even in a future reincarnation. This sudden realization of her true identity must have brought her ecstasy. At the same time she was aware that others might find it puzzling. For this reason she would not let the landlord Mengzhan see her poems. Yet her joy in this state of being was an all encompassing experience; it needed to be told and so she committed it to her poetry.

It was after gaining this awareness of her own self-worth that He Shuangqing was confronted by a farm woman, asking her why she did not commit suicide in view of her wretched fate (see translation on pp. 89–90). In consideration of the woman's level of understanding, He Shuangqing casually said that it was a matter of having to repay some debts incurred in her previous life. This being a tenet of Buddhism, it was an acceptable answer to the farm woman. However, it in no way reflects He Shuangqing's own understanding as to why she would not capitulate to what social convention expected her to do. She went on to comfort her friend by saying that in relative terms her situation was not the worst there was. Then she analyzed her life for the woman with honesty and in broad strokes by saying, "People say I am ill-fated, but that's because they think I have talent and beauty. After all, there are many untalented and ordinary looking girls around, they too would like to have good husbands. I am not alone in this wish." Here, as elsewhere, her concern for others enabled her to keep the right perspective before her and, therefore, she maintained the ability to face her life with realistic calm. This generosity of heart gave her peace of mind. It strengthened her faith and lifted her towards transcendent enlightenment.

In her "Colophon for the Painting 'Planting Melons' " written to the tune of *Yujing qiu* (see translation on pp. 56–57), she had unabashedly asked, "Who is concerned about me, / A goddess of flowers / Exiled temporarily on earth?" In her new state she told her friend, "Beauty and talent are given to me by Heaven to destroy me. If I should commit suicide to carry out the wish of Heaven, I'd be very foolish indeed." In other words, her new awareness had enabled her to see through the notion of fate subscribed to by her society. She would have nothing to do with that notion, since she was not responsible for it in the first place. That being the case, she readily challenged society and even Heaven by transcending both. For it was this realization that made her openly advise those who would learn from her example to first "not to blame themselves."

More on He Shuangqing's new awareness of her self-worth can be detected in her subsequent letter to her uncle, even though she did not mention it as such in that letter, because she knew her Confucian uncle would not understand this in a woman (see translation on p. 91). She valued human relationships and so she skillfully worked her real message between the lines. Having realized in her own mind that she was not responsible for her fate, she started the letter with: "Everybody [including her uncle" says it is my fate to be cast into such miserable circumstances," but she corrected this by saying, "Actually my life is not that miserable." Calmly she put the picture into a broad perspective by citing the sad experiences of many young women confined to the inner chambers of rich households, in contrast to her own unconfined condition in the countryside. She called them "bright pearls cast into black waters" and "fragrant orchids that are regarded as worthless things." She then turned to her lines on the chrysanthemum and the lonely wild goose (see pp. 76–77 and 78–79), which many people, especially Confucians, had interpreted as a sign of resentment on her part. At this point we can imagine how she must grieve to see her empathy with her subjects being thus distorted. Nevertheless, in consideration of her uncle, she accepted the responsibility for perhaps being resentful insofar as she was human and, therefore, capable of such a failing. But knowing full well that the charge of resentment was directed at her relationship with her husband, she made this positive statement, "Yet I know I do not resent my husband." This was the truth, since in her state of transcendence she had just recorded her feelings for her husband in her "Nine Poems Harmonizing Bailuo." In conclusion, she humored her uncle with something he wanted to hear, "... I only want to become a man in my next life." But her real message was in the last line of "I shall be content to spend the rest of my life in *Chan* 禪[44] meditation and chanting Buddhist hymns." These were indeed her wishes; they are steps toward ultimate enlightenment whether one were male or female that a Confucian could understand, and so she did not hesitate to open her heart about them to her uncle.

Like Shi Zhenlin, He Shuangqing had a Confucian upbringing but embraced Daoism and Buddhism intellectually and spiritually. Her Daoist transcendence propelled her onto the path of *Chan* Buddhist enlightenment without her being consciously aware of it. For, no sooner had she written to her uncle than she wrote "After Ningxi's Rhyme," in which she leaped easily from Poem II, where she announced "My abode is in Huayang's [Daoist's] Eighth heaven," to Poem V, where she surrenders her ego-personality and removes herself from personal ambition saying "The scholars came to appreciate talent / But received little response from me;/Now I'm peacefully/Settled in a farm family." Unmistakably, this abandonment from worldly ambitions are the initial steps toward enlightenment.

Zhuangzi[45] argued for the search of the Dao (the Way) when he said: "When the pond dries up and fish are left on the dry bed, rather than leave them to moisten one another with their spittle, it would be better to let them lose themselves in their native rivers and lakes. Rather than praise Yao and blame Jie (the virtuous and the wicked), it would be better to forget both and lose oneself in the Dao."[46] He Shuangqing understood this. She did not blame anyone, including herself, for her misfortune; rather, she forgot about the virtuous and the wicked and concentrated on her transcendence. This philosophical approach to her restricted life preserved her good disposition and nurtured her creativity in servitude, elevating her above the daily stress and strain and helping her look at life with detached realism.

Her broad perspective coupled with detached realism gave her strength and courage to take the right actions regardless of society's proscriptions. This explains why, as much as she observed chastity and womanly decorum, she transcended a social taboo when she sent her work to Shi Zhenlin for inclusion in his notebook and engaged in literary communications with the scholars. Being motivated by compassion, He Shuangqing's consideration for others, as for example, her offer to pad Yuhan's suit with quilting, often became the neighbors' gossip. Yet she would not let such pettiness deter her from doing what she deemed was right. She openly faced her neighbor to say: "I am not an ordinary country woman, hiding from good people and relatives to keep company with only the lowly. I am open, sincere, I am not secretive in my actions. I don't admire lovers who dig holes in walls to meet one another" (see translation on p. 107). Then, on the occasion when Shi Zhenlin wanted to destroy his *Sanji* manuscript in one of his depressed moods, He Shuangqing took it upon herself to write him, urging him to match his words with action (see translation on p. 112). Her letter shows a maturity beyond her years. As a matter of fact, through that letter we catch a glimpse of He Shuangqing's early maturity in her penetrating evaluation of her uncle's self-deceptive moralizing when she was only fifteen years old.

He Shuangqing had faith in her Goddess of Mercy in whose

compassionate example she lived. This was the ladder to her enlightenment. For example, it was her compassion that explains her composure toward abusive treatment when her mother-in-law caught her gazing at a wild goose landing on an embankment and suspected that she was trying to dodge work by watching the bird. Although shaken, she did not let her mother-in-law's attitude interfere with her concern over the bird, which inspired the poem, "The Lonely Wild Goose" written to the tune of *Xi huanghua man* (see translation on pp. 78–79). Were it not for Shi Zhenlin's recording of the unhappy intrusion, we would not know from her poem of this abuse. Likewise, when she was locked in the woodshed by her husband for pleading with him to stop gambling, she simply let his mistreatment of her pass without letting it disturb her compassionate identification with the smoldering lampwick in her poem, "The Dying Lamp Wick" written to the tune of *Fenghuang taishang yi chuixiao* (see translation on p. 96).

What super-human capacity helped He Shuangqing maintain her disposition, compassion and creativity until the very end of her distressing life? Deprived as she was, what vision enabled her to identify with all animate life and be constantly concerned with its well being? To what degree did she attain enlightenment? Did she attain the realization of her original Buddha-nature or nirvana? Answers to such questions about our poet can only be found in her life and work. I hope that my translation will provide a life-example of a poet who lived the quest for enlightenment without being conscious of its process. If it is useful to those interested in the eternal question of human existence, I am certain that He Shuangqing would be more than pleased that her life had indeed not been lived in vain.

Insofar as eighteenth-century China was concerned, He Shuangqing was but a farmwife in the countryside. However, her poetic expression made it clear to Shi Zhenlin and his friends that, like themselves, she had creativity, heavily burdened as she was. Their sympathy for her unhappy condition opened their eyes to the social strictures dictating women's lives. Although the bolder of Shi's friends vaunted convention to openly offer their friendship to our poet, their frustration over the irrationality of so-called fate that allowed the institution of arranged marriage to ruin the lives of many young women like He Shuangqing, was difficult for them to assuage. They also questioned the prudish separation of the two sexes, especially in literary fellowship. In the end they respected and even admired He Shuangqing for her leap toward transcendence, but they continued to harbor a feeling of distress toward life in general, and social decrees in particular.

He Shuangqing's death around 1737, while the scholars were away in the capital following their imperial examination, was not recorded in *Xiqing sanji*. But readers are forewarned as the scholars mentally prepared themselves to accept He Shuangqing's choice of transcendence. The poet's death at a time when the examination propelled her scholar friends into a career shift, called for an end to the *Sanji*. For when Shi Zhenlin came home after receiving his *jinshi* degree, he faced a void left by her death that was never again to be filled. This applied to all the scholars who used to meet at Jintan as a coterie and were drawn by He Shuangqing as a cause célèbre. The brevity of her life had brought them face to face with social reflection; her achievement in spiritual transcendence had set an example for them to search for in their own destinies. From now on they entered a new phase of their lives, for they could never remain the same after their experience of watching her rise like a radiant vision from a farmer's abode only to vanish behind the darkness of their own sorrow at her passing. They needed to dispel this sadness by recalling her admirable qualities. Very likely this was one of the reasons why the *Xiqing sanji* was put into print soon after with the help of one of Shi's friends, Wu Zhensheng 吳震生 or the Yugou

Lyric Poet (玉勾詞客),[47] who happened to be another admirer of He Shuangqing's character (see translation on p. 132).

In his later years Shi Zhenlin remained attached to his *Xiqing sanji*, referring to it time and time again in his *Huayang sangao*. It was said that he revised it to delete twenty percent of its contents when he was eighty-seven, the year before he died.[48] If a copy of that edition could be found, it would be interesting to see what he regarded as being irrelevant forty-three years after the book's first publication. I have a feeling that no matter what he deleted, He Shuangqing's life and work would be preserved.

It has been suggested by some that He Shuangqing could have been a figment of Shi Zhenlin's imagination and that he could have written the poetry attributed to her, as has been true with some scholars who have written lyric songs for their favorite courtesans and signed the women's names to them. From this we can see that the records of He Shuangqing are indeed so exceptional that she invites conjectures even today, just as she did in her own days, according to Shi Zhenlin.

In my mind there can be no doubt that she existed. In the first place, she is recorded in the county records of Danyang and Jintan, no matter how briefly. In the second place, her poetry is extremely feminine; its tenor, its contents, and its colors are straight from the heart of a young woman in the sort of disgraceful life situation in which our poet found herself after her marriage. In the third place, the sensitivity in her work could not be faked by even the most sympathetic male. Fourth, if Shi Zhenlin had wanted to write an imaginary story, he could have written and acknowledged a fictional one. The fact is that his writings show him to be open, sincere, honest and sensitive to the feelings of others, with a certain amount of the detachment essential for a good objective biographer, though not a fiction writer. From his two notebooks we can see that he was interested in people and made it his life-long vocation to write sketches and portraits of them. He Shuangqing happened to be the largest canvas that he did, since she provided him with insightful material from both her life and work until she died. In a sense, her portrait was unfinished in his writings, but therein lies the real meaning or triumph of her life. Furthermore, Shi Zhenlin had no reason to fabricate He Shuangqing when many of his friends involved themselves in her life; and he certainly would not have portrayed his special friends, Anshu and Yuhan, in their infatuation for his own amusement. Finally, as recorded in his *Huayang sangao*, there are letters[49] he wrote to some of these friends that refer to He Shuangqing's passing as something they all mourned.

* * *

Women poets go back to the beginning of the poetic tradition in Chinese history under the emerging society of the early Zhou dynasty (1122–255 B.C.). They authored many of the love songs found in the first poetry anthology, *Shi jing* 詩經 .[50] still extant. Theirs were among the poems recommended by Confucius (551–479 B.C.), who encouraged his disciples to read this poetry collection. However, soon after that, later Confucian strictures put women under the domination of men, robbing them of all leisure and education, and instilling into their lives a set of "virtues" that centered on obedience, service, the effacement of identity, and the hiding of their talents behind what was deemed as propriety. As a result, women poets in later ages were few and far between. Generally, those whose works have been preserved were from the elite and the courtesan classes. As for other writers who were fortunate to have acquired an education by themselves, they were not taken seriously and their work was often destroyed after they died, leaving whatever was handed down to be found only in private collections. It was rare for common women to have an education, let alone to become poets. Equally uncommon were sympathetic males who would lend support to women seeking knowledge, unless they were from within the family. He Shuangqing's story is thus rare in Chinese literature, and so is Shi Zhenlin's record of an otherwise unknown woman.

Fortunately, the trust He Shuangqing had in Shi Zhenlin to record her work was well placed, since Shi was sensitive, yet objective and open-minded. Furthermore, he had the interest and far-sightedness to record her life in addition to her work. Only this combined record could help others understand in depth the poet as a person, to grasp her achievement in a life that was short and restrictive, and to appreciate her calm dignity and independent vision.

Therefore, the aim of this translation is twofold: to bring to the present the life and work of a farmwife from eighteenth-century China and to recognize Shi Zhenlin, as well as his friends, for championing humanity through their respect for the oppressed and their promotion of talent without discrimination on the grounds of social status or gender. Inasmuch as the Qing scholar and poet, Yuan Mei 袁枚 (1716–1798), is recognized as the first to openly encourage women poets[51] by accepting some of them as his students during his seventies, it should be noted that Shi Zhenlin's *Xiqing sanji* preceded Yuan Mei's action by more than half a century.

Though tedious at times, the work of translation is a joy when the translator feels a kinship with the subject. He Shuangqing touched me profoundly when I first learned about her, and Shi Zhenlin spoke to me as a writer of humility and trustworthiness. If my translation can put across the insight that a farmwife in eighteenth-century China had over adversity, I believe that both He Shuangqing and Shi Zhenlin would be satisfied. They were peaceful souls and the goodwill they worked so hard to share with others during their lives should not be forgotten.

A translator encounters many unexpected surprises when digging into the history, folklore and human factors behind the material. This occurs in even straightforward matters like place names. Through the long history of China with its many dynastic changes, some of the place names have changed several times for political, social or economic reasons. Adding to the confusion is the fact that the earlier names have been often used by Chinese writers, especially poets, for their historic flavor. Take for example, the city of Yangzhou 揚州, where no less than five of the six names[52] that it has garnered since its founding in the third century B.C. are used in *Xiqing sanji*, without any clue that they refer to the same city. Another example is Piling 毗陵, where, according to Shi Zhenlin, many women sought He Shuangqing's poetry from him during one of his visits there (see translation on p. 126). I spent countless hours tracking this city on maps and in county records and gazetteers. Finally, a fine combing of an old provincial chorography[53] revealed that Piling was founded in the Han dynasty (206 B.C.–A.D. 220) and that it is today's Changzhou 常州, also called Lanling 蘭陵 or Wujin 武進. It is also important to keep in mind that Shi Zhenlin was a native of this area. His intimate knowledge of the local towns and their institutions (such as shrines) explains the casualness with which he treats their names in his journal. As a matter of fact, some of the places in his book are small villages, as for example, He Shuangqing's home of Jiangshu, Danyang and Xiaoshan, Jintan. The former is traced to the southeast of Danyang on an ancient map, while we can only guess that Xiaoshan is located in western Jintan where it touches the foothills of the Mao Shan 茅山 (Mao Range).

This brings up a historical fact of interest, which though obscure, is nevertheless the pride of the natives in this area, as can be seen in their local records. It was recorded that in the third century B.C. the First Emperor of Qin, upon hearing that this area had a "kingly air" in its atmosphere, acted by sending in three thousand prisoner-laborers dressed in red uniform to gouge a furrow through the mountain range from Zhenjiang down to Danyang, bending it at the latter place to redirect and dispel that threatening "air."[54] For this reason, Zhenjiang's initial name was changed to Dantu 丹徒 or "Prisoner-laborers in Red" after the incident, and Danyang was called Qu-A 曲阿 (or Crooked Ridge) when it was founded at that time. The defacement of the mountain range could have extended all the way to Xiaoshan, Jintan, since Xiaoshan itself means "To Destroy Mountain." The excavation could also have extended westward to include Mao Shan, as it was named Juqu 句曲 (or Crooked Bent Mountain) in the Han dynasty which succeeded the Qin dynasty. Only the passing of time has allowed nature to heal these wounds and diffuse the memory of the people such that two thousand years later Shi Zhenlin would record Anshu's laudatory remarks about the mountain scenery around Xiaoshan (see translation on p. 68).

Records of He Shuangqing, together with materials relevant to her, make up twenty-two percent of *Xiqing sanji*. Interspersed throughout the book, they are sometimes written as vignettes and other times as strict records. In addition to these materials, I have translated a few other passages from Shi's writing to shed light on the world of a Chinese scholar, a world that He Shuangqing shared mentally and spiritually even when she was excluded from it socially. The purpose for this is to make He Shuangqing's story intelligible and coherent and to bring out Shi Zhenlin's way of life, the quality of his writing, and his character as a person. As the entries in the book take the form of untitled essays, and as they are written chronologically and grouped into four chapters that also lack titles, I have given captions to the translated passages to bring out their salient features.

He Shuangqing's poetry comes in both the regulated rhymed, four- and eight-line verse (詩 *shi*) and the rhymed lyric style (詞 *ci*). The latter was her forte. In contrast to the regulated style, the lyric verse is subject to more intricate rules of tone discipline and has to follow the measures of lyric tunes, by which it is sung.

For this reason, while a tune title is kept as the model for a lyric poem, it is not to be confused with the title of the poem itself. For example, her lyric verse written to the tune of *Yujing qiu* 玉京秋 has "Colophon for the Painting 'Planting Melons'" as the poem's own title. This lyric style is an exacting art that demands a fine-tuned, musical ear and a poetic sensitivity, even as it accomodates colloquialism. All this our poet had command of at her finger tips. Instinctively she used these facilities in their various nuances to express in her poetry the very pulse of her heart as it moved into transcendence. In so doing, she found solace in a beauty that still speaks to us through her work today.

It should be remembered that traditional Chinese poetry is always rhymed. In translation, however, this is generally sacrificed for the main tasks of adhering to the spirit and feeling of the poet, and of the Chinese language, while rendering its English version readable. Therefore, He Shuangqing's poetry in translation may appear to be free verse, but it is important to remember that in its original Chinese, it is rhymed.

For readers who want to explore the art of Chinese traditional poetry, an excellent reference is *The Art of Chinese Poetry* by James J. Y. Liu.[55] In this book, Liu goes into the Chinese language as a medium of poetic expression, points out some Chinese concepts and ways of thinking and feeling, then surveys traditional Chinese views on poetry to arrive at a synthesis on the art of Chinese poetry. Throughout, attention is given to the translation of Chinese poetry into the English language for Western ears.

He Shuangqing's poetry is assembled at the back of the book, with its translation and its original Chinese text on opposite pages.

Notes

1. See the epilogue by the publisher Zhang Jinglu 張靜盧 in Shi Zhenlin's *Xiqing sanji* (*Zhongguo wenxue zhenben congshu* 中國文學珍本叢書 [Collections of Rare Manuscripts From Chinese Literature], first collection, no. 5) (Shanghai: Shanghai zazhi gongsi, 1935), p. 212. All page references to *Xiqing sanji* are to this edition.
2. The form of divination used by the scholars was that of *fuji* 扶亂 (see *Xiqing sanji*, pp. 6, 10, 17). The procedure entails two participants supporting a stick, one at each end. From the center of the stick is suspended another piece of wood with a stylus at its tip, and the whole apparatus is placed over a pan of sand. The process commences with reverential concentration by the participants to invite the spirit of the deceased; then the spirit's arrival is made known by the stylus moving on its own accord. The participants put their questions to the spirit verbally, and the latter responds by writing out his or her answers on the sand. This is concluded by the formality of thanking and bidding goodbye to the spirit.
3. See the two letters to Yugou Lyric Poet 玉勾詞客 and the condolence letter to Cao Zhenting 曹震亭 in Shi Zhenlin's *Huayang sangao* 華陽散稿 [Huayang Essays] (*Zhongguo wenxue zhenben congshu*, first collection, no. 9) (Shanghai: Shanghai zazhi gongsi, 1935), pp. 15–17.
4. Gao Shi 高士, "Boming nu shiren — He Shuangqing" 薄命女詩人 — 賀雙卿 [The Ill-fated Poet, He Shuangqing], *Tiansheng bao* 天聲報 (San Francisco), 19 September 1978.
5. Contrary to the European practice of boarding an infant with a wet nurse in her home, in China a wet nurse would leave her own baby at home to be taken care of by a relative and hire herself out to take care of her employer's baby in their home. The European way spelled high mortality for infants given to the care of wet nurses. The Chinese way provided close supervision and special nutrition for the nurse by the employer. With this practice in mind, I feel that the bad temper of Farmer Zhou might have resulted from whatever neglect he suffered during his infancy when his mother worked as a

wet nurse away from him. Sometimes a wet nurse to the rich and powerful in China became part of the family for life through her role as a mother surrogate, thus acquiring respect and even power over her charge as the latter grew up. (See reference to Wanjuan's wet nurse in translation, "The Daughters of Jin Baiyan.").

6. Beginning with Liu Xiang 劉向 of the Former Han dynasty (206 B.C.–A.D. 23), many self-appointed guardians of morality wrote injunctions for the edification of Chinese women. These injunctions took various forms, ranging from biographies of historic model women to actual commandments that spelled out the details of women's daily life and conduct.
7. Liu Xiang 劉向, *Lienu zhuan* (Biographies of Women) written in the Former Han dynasty, in 30 B.C. The edition I used was illustrated by Chou Jiuzhou of the Ming dynasty and was reprinted by Guangwen Publishing Co. in Taipei in 1978.
8. Lu Xun 魯迅 (1881–1936) was a great writer of modern China. His life spanned the declining years of the Qing dynasty and the civil war years of the Chinese Republic before the Japanese invasion of 1937. A progressive and dedicated thinker, he helped launch the May Fourth Movement and was a prolific writer whose aim was to raise the consciousness of the Chinese people.
9. Lu Xun, "My Views on Chastity," in *Silent China: Selected Writings of Lu Xun*, edited and translated by Gladys Yang (Oxford: Oxford University Press, 1973), pp. 141–43.
10. Dong Jiazun 董家遵, "Lidai jielie funu di tongji" 歷代節烈婦女的統計 [An Estimation of the Number of Women Who Remained Unmarried and Who Committed Suicide After Their Husbands' Death], in *Zhongguo funu shilun ji* 中國婦女史論集 [Annotations on Women in Chinese History], edited by Bao Jialin 鮑家麟 (Taipei: Mutong chubanshe 牧童出版社, 1979), pp. 111–17.

    According to Dong, data for the Song dynasty (300 years) on women who remained unmarried and who committed suicide after their husbands' death is 100 percent above that for all previous dynasties combined, or for 2000 years altogether. From the Song dynasty through the Qing dynasty, each dynasty's data on such women escalated over that of the previous one. Dong's statistics for the Qing dynasty had to be extrapolated, since it was gathered from "Brave Women" in *han* 函 41–43, *ce* 冊 398–404, *juan* 卷 45–118, and "Chaste Women" in *han* 43–45, *ce* 404–20, *juan* 119–328 of *Gujin tushu jicheng* 古今圖書集成 [The Encyclopedia of Chinese Works From Early Times to the Present (i.e. 1725)]. *Gujin tushu jicheng* was first compiled by Chen Menglei 陳夢雷 and later by Jiang Tingxi 莊廷錫 *et al.* with imperial approval. It was completed in 1725. The most readily available edition being the Zhonghua shuju 中華書局 edition which is a reprint, in 1934, of the 1728 edition.

This means that the data for Qing dynasty apply to only the first eighty years of its 267 years. When extrapolated to cover the entire 267 years, the result shows the highest number of women who either remained unmarried or committed suicide after their husbands' death in Chinese history.

11. County records in China (縣志 *xian zhi*), together with gazetteers (方志 *fang zhi*), are a vast class of writings that record the statistics of the locality. The extent of these records, and their systematic comprehensiveness is probably unrivalled in the world, says Joseph Needham, quoting Alexander Wylie, in his *Science and Civilisation in China*, Vol. I (Cambridge: Cambridge University Press, 1954), p. 120. He traces their beginning to the fourth century A.D. He says that according to Carrington Goodrich, "One after another of these local records were compiled, sometimes as a labor of love by a retired scholar of the district, sometimes by official order to provide all the information about the local government for which there came a succession of men from the outside." These county records contain: tax data, records tracing the genealogy of the people and materials from the history and geography of the district, a chronicle with listings of their institutions and monuments, rosters of their famous sons, martyrs, hermits and monks. Special attention was given to natural calamities and "strange" happenings. Since they were written by the literati, the more ambitious compilations would include literary works written about the locality, local authors of both men and women with notes on their lives and titles of their works. They usually end with a

list of "chaste and brave" women, whose "virtuous" deeds in remaining unmarried or committing suicide after their husbands' death, or whose filial acts were deemed to reflect the morality of the district. Significantly, these records are treasured by the native sons. For this reason many of them have been reprinted in Taiwan for compatriots of the districts who have moved to Taiwan with the Nationalists from mainland China since the establishment of the People's Republic of China.

12. Yang Qi 楊棨, *Jiangsu sheng: Jingkou shanshui zhi* 江蘇省：京口山水志 (Topographies of Jingkou, Jiangsu Province), in *Zhongguo fangzhi congshu* 中國方志叢書 [Topographies of China Series]: *Huazhong difang* 華中地方 (Central China), No. 6 (Taipei: Chengwen chubanshe 成文出版社 reprint of the 1844 edition, 1970), pp. 24–25. (Note: Jingkou includes Dantu or present-day Zhenjiang, Danyang, Jintan and Liyang.)
13. *Danyang xianzhi* 丹陽縣志 [County Records of Danyang] (Taipei: Huaxin yinshuguan 華新印書館, 1961).
14. *Jintan xianzhi* 金壇縣志 [County Records of Jintan], 2 vols. (Taipei: Jinshi yinzhi youxian gongsi 金氏印製有限公司, 1971). Reproduced from the 1921 revision by former residents of the Jintan association residing in Taiwan.
15. *Danyang xianzhi, juan* 35, p. 33.
16. See the chapter entitled "Virtuous and Good," *Jintan xianzhi*, Vol. II, *juan* 10, p. 4.
17. Wang Yunzhang 王蘊章 (ed.), *Ranzhi yuyun* 然脂餘韻 [Rhymes Recovered From Women Writers] (Shanghai: Shangwu yinshuguan 商務印書館, 1918).
18. There are three poetry anthologies containing He Shuangqing's work, published before 1932 and after the Qing dynasty:
    (1) Xu Ke 徐珂 (ed.), *Lidai guixiu cixuan jiping* 歷代閨秀詞選集評 [Selections and Critique of Women's Lyric Verses Through the Ages] (Shanghai: Shangwu yinshuguan, 1926).
    (2) Wu Hao 吳灝 (ed.), *Lidai mingyuan cixuan* 歷代名媛詞選 [Lyric Verses From Chinese Women Through the Ages] (Shanghai: Mushi shanfang 木石山房, n.d.).

(3) Li Baiying 李白英 (ed.), *Zhongguo lidai nuzi cixuan* 中國歷代女子詞選 [Selections From Women's Lyric Verses Through the Ages] (Shanghai: Guanghua shuju 光華書局, 1932).

19. The three anthologies containing He Shuangqing's work, published between 1961 and 1978 are:
    (1) Tong Renlan 童紉蘭 and Sun Peicai 孫佩茝 (eds.), *Nu zuojia shici xuan* 女作家詩詞選 [Selections of Poetry by Women Writers] (Hong Kong: Lezhi chubanshe 樂知出版社, 1961).
    (2) Yi Baiyin 裔柏蔭 (ed.), *Lidai nu shici xuan* 歷代女詩詞選 [Selections of Women's Poetry Through the Ages] (Taipei: Dangdai tushu chubanshe 當代圖書出版社, 1971).
    (3) Nai Ding 乃鼎 (ed.), *Sushou yin* 素手吟 [The Hums of Women] (Taipei: Nanjing chuban gongsi 南京出版公司, 1978). In this book, He Shuangqing's work was mistakenly placed in the Song dynasty.
20. Han Shiqiu 韓石秋, *Qingdai wenxue shi* 清代文學史 [History of the Literature of the Qing Dynasty] (Gaoxiong, Taiwan: Baicheng shuju 百成書局, 1973), pp. 189–92. Han reaffirmed that the best woman lyric poets in Chinese history was Li Qingzhao 李清照 of the Song dynasty. For him the major women lyric poets in the Qing dynasty were: He Shuangqing (1715–?), Wu Zao (吳藻, 1796–?) and Lü Bicheng (呂碧成, 1884–1943).
21. See preface of their book (p. 3) for lines quoted by the authors from He Shuangqing's "Nine Poems Harmonizing Bailuo" that were used as examples of hypocritical writing by women.
    Poem II: "Since I can preserve the padded jacket / To keep my husband warm, / My heart is like honey, / I don't reject him."
    Poem III: "The sudden chill in the night / Is accompanied by a fierce wind — / Don't blow at my husband, / Concentrate on me."
22. "Harmonizing" means using the same rhyme. If the harmony is done using the same rhyme without following the order, it is called "using the same rhyme"; if it is done using the same rhyme in the same order, it is called "following the same rhyme." This started in the Tang dynasty and became popular in the Song dynasty, when it was made into a game of skill.

23. See preface of their book (p. 5) for lines quoted to illustrate the genuine and soulful qualities in women's poetry.
Poem IV: "I pick weeds for greens, / In the cold I wash them; / The chrysanthemum may suffer, / What can you do about the frost?"
Poem V: "My life is fragile / Like a cicada's wing. / I used to be as beautiful / As the neighbor's daughter — / When Mother sees me, / Will she recognize her child / Now that bitter yellow has robbed / My face of its cheerful pink?"
Poem VI: "Deluged by spring's tempering / Is my little heart; / In illness dreams are infrequent — / They fade easily. / Having pawned my mirror, / Gold hairpins to buy medicine, / I must whittle some willow branches / To pin up my hair by the reflection of the water."
24. See preface (p. 3): "To alleviate the emptiness of her family life, He Shuangqing relied on her poetry to express her depression. She even communicated with some so-called scholars."
25. Wang Fanting 王藩庭, *Zhonghua lidai funu* 中華歷代婦女 [Chinese Women Through the Ages] (Taipei: Shangwu yinshuguan, 1966), pp. 311–415.
26. The two references from Zhang Shoulin's edition of He Shuangqing's *Xueya xuan ji* that cannot be found are: Bai Yang 拜鴦, *Qianchou ji* 欠愁集 [Collection of Debts Owed] and Wang Yunshan 王韻珊, *Guochao cizhong xubian* 國朝詞綜續編 [Supplement to Qing Poetry].
27. Xu Naichang 徐乃昌, *Xiaotanluan shi huike guixiu shiji* 小檀欒室彙刻閨秀十集 [Ten Volumes of Women's Collected Works From the Xiaotanluan shi Studio]. This book turned out to be a supplement to Xu's *Baijia ci* 百家詞 (Lyric Verses by One Hundred Poets). Zhang Shoulin wrote that Xu followed Wang Yunshan's *Guochao cizhong xubian* in using *Xueya xuan ji* as the title of He Shuangqing's poetry collection, and that Xu recorded this in his supplementary volume. Xu's supplement yields no poetry by He Shuangqing, but its preface indicates that his *Baijia ci* would be the right reference. However, I was not able to find it in the United States.
28. Dong Chao 董潮 (Dongting 東亭), "Donggao zachao" 東皐雜鈔 in Wu Shenglan's 吳省蘭 *Yihai zhuchen* 藝海珠塵 (Taipei, 1968), *juan* 3, p. 6. Here He Shuangqing's name was given as Zhang Qingqing 張慶青.

She was reported to be a farmer's wife who was a self-made poet and who did not resent being married to a farmer. The story was told of a salt merchant who tried to woo her but was rebuffed by her. Two of her lyric verses were mentioned: "Lonely Wild Goose" written to the tune of *Xi huanghua man* and "The Dying Lamp Wick" written to the tune of *Fenghuang tai shang yi chuixiao*.

29. The four extra poems found in Shi Zhenlin's *Xiqing sanji* are: "The Frog" (咏蛙), "The Plantain" (苿苜), "The Heavenly Bamboo" (天竹子), and "Snow Clearing Over the Western Mountains" (西山雪霽).
30. See *Jintan xianzhi*:
    (1) Vol. I, *juan* 8, p. 7: "Shi Zhenlin passed the imperial examination in 1736."
    (2) "Literature," Vol. II, *juan* 9, pp. 8–9: for a summary of Shi's life.
    (3) Vol. II, *juan* 11, p. 3: *Xiqing sanji* is listed under "Novelists" (小説家類) by mistake.
31. *Xiqing sanji*, p. 1.
32. *Ibid.*, p. 51.
33. *Ibid.*, p. 97.
34. The grandfather of Wu Wang 武王 , who founded the Zhou dynasty (12th cent.–3rd cent. B.C.), was Tai Wang 太王 , a feudal prince under the Shang 商 dynasty (18th cent.–12 cent. B.C.). He had three sons, Taibo 泰伯, Zhongyong 仲雍 and Jili 季歷. Jili had a son named Chang 昌 . Tai Wang once remarked, "If our family should ever prosper, it may rest on the shoulders of Chang." Upon hearing this, the eldest son knew that his father wished to hand down his title to their third brother so that the latter's son, Chang, could inherit it. Consequently, he and his second brother exiled themselves to the then uncivilized land south of the Yangzi River and lived among the primitive settlers, tattooing themselves and cutting off their hair as a declaration of their resolve. The native people were touched by their unselfishness. They made Taibo their leader over Juwu, which was then Jiangsu province and later included Jiejiang and southern Shandong provinces.
35. The ancient kingdoms are Wu 吳, Yue 越 and Chu 楚. Wu dates back

to at least sixth century B.C. but was conquered by Yue in 473 B.C., and Yue, in turn, was taken by Chu in 334 B.C.

36. See *The Travels of Marco Polo*, edited by Ernest Rhys (London: J. M. Dent & Sons, 1921), pp. 291–310.
37. See Shi Zhenlin, "Epilogue for *Huayun xuan yi gao*" (花韻軒遺稿跋), in his *Huayang sangao*, p. 71.
38. "County Professor" (教諭 *jiaoyu*) was a professorial office in charge of instructing the bureaucracy serving the county government. According to the *Jintan xianzhi*, Vol. II, pp. 615–16, Shi Zhenlin lived by the golden rule as an example for the officials he was to instruct when he was County Professor at Huai'an. For example, when the Pin River (瀕水) overflowed and drowned many people in 1748, he contributed all his savings for their burial.
39. *Jintan xianzhi*, Vol. II, *juan* 9, p. 8.
40. *Jinshi* 進士 was a third and final degree graduate in the old Chinese civil service system. Its examination was administered at the capital, hence it was called the imperial examination.
41. In old China, girls were separated from the boys, including their own brothers. They were kept in an inner chamber or area for their womanly education. This consisted of the "four virtues": womanly virtues or the discipline of hiding one's talents, being gentle, kind, well mannered, being respectful; womanly conversation or the art of keeping quiet and speaking only when spoken to; womanly appearance or the art of keeping oneself and one's clothing clean, having the proper demeanor in one's posture; womanly industry, the learning of silk culture and various kinds of weaving, sewing and embroidery and preparation of sacrificial foods for ancestral worship for the men in the clan. They seldom ventured out of this chamber area, the only exception being the farmer's daughters and wives, whose help was needed in the farm.
42. The *Xin jing* (Heart sutra) is one of the sutras that are collections of sermons, chiefly given by the Buddha. According to William Edward Soothill and Lewis Roduns' *A Dictionary of Chinese Buddhist Terms with Sanskrit and English Equivalents* (London: Kegan Paul, Trench, Trubner & Co., 1934), p. 151. The *Xin jing* is considered to be

"divinely distributed" (神分心經) when publicly recited to get rid of evil spirits.

43. See the *Cihai* 辭海 on "Poetry on Red Leaves" (紅葉題詩): There are at least three stories at different periods of the Tang dynasty about court ladies whose poetry, written on red leaves, floated out of the imperial grounds through the sewers and were picked up by the individuals whom these ladies married afterwards upon their release from court service.
44. *Chan* 禪 is a Buddhist sect that originated in India and was introduced into China in the sixth century A.D. It emerged as Chinese *Chan* Buddhism (禪宗) in the seventh century when Chinese thinkers were ready to go beyond logic, metaphysics and psychology to a more direct confrontation of reality. Its emphasis is on meditation and its goal is sudden enlightenment. It flourished all over China from the seventh century until the thirteenth century, and has been continued in Japan as Zen Buddhism since its inception there in the twelfth century. See the Foreword by Chang Chung-yuan in his *Teachings of Chan Buddhism* (New York: Pantheon Press, 1969), pp. vii–x.
45. Zhuangzi 莊子 (369–286 B.C.) was a Daoist philosopher.
46. Lin Yutang 林語堂 (ed.), *The Wisdom of Laotse* (New York: Modern Library, 1948), p. 45. In this book Lin Yutang uses Zhuangzi's text to explain Laozi's Daoism.
47. See Shi Zhenlin's preface in his *Huayang sangao*, p. 3.
48. See the epilogue by Zhang Jinglu, in Shi Zhenlin's *Xiqing sanji*, p. 212.
49. For references to He Shuangqing's death, see Shi Zhenlin's *Huayang sangao*, p. 15, in his letter to Yugou Cike and letter to Cao Zhenting.
50. The *Shi jing* 詩經 , or *Book of Poetry* or *The Odes*, is a collection of rhymed ballads composed from the reign of Yu 禹 (22nd cent. B.C.) to the beginning of the sixth century B.C. They numbered 305 and were believed to be culled from 3,000 by Confucius. They fall into four categories: (1) ballads from various feudal states under the reign of the Son of Heaven. These were collected from various feudal states, selectively put into music by the court musicians to serve as a

"barometer" on the quality of the local administration; (2) odes sung for court entertainments; (3) odes sung on special occasions when the feudal nobles gathered; and (4) sacrificial odes. Many of the love songs in the first group were composed by women.

51. The women students of Yuan Mei 袁枚 were called "Suiyuan's Women Disciples" (隨園女弟子), Suiyuan 隨園 being the pen name of Yuan Mei and also the name of his estate in Nanjing where he lived and taught after retiring early from court service.

52. Initially called Weiyang 惟揚, then changed to Weiyang written with a different character for the first word (維揚), the city then had the successive names of Guangling 廣陵 , Jiangdu 江都 and Hancheng 邗城 before it became Yangzhou 揚州. In his *Xiqing sanji*, Shi Zhenlin used five of the above names for the same city in various places: Weiyang 惟揚 on pp. 139 and 149; Guangling on pp. 44 and 183; Hancheng on p. 150; Jiangdu on pp. 183 and 185; and Yangzhou on pp. 97, 150 and 185.

    For further reference, see: (1) *Cihai* 辭海 , "Weiyang" 維揚 ; and (2) *Jiangsu sheng: Jiangsu quan sheng yutu* 江蘇省 ：江蘇全省輿圖 (Maps of Jiangsu Province), compiled by Zhu Kebao 諸可寶 of the Qing dynasty, in *Zhongguo fangzhi congshu* 中國方志叢書 (Topographies of China Series): *Huazhong difang* 華中地方 (Central China), No. 144 (Taipei: Chengwen chubanshe 成文出版社 reprint of the 1844 edition, 1974), pp. 164–65.

53. *Jiangsu quan sheng yutu*, pp. 365–67.

54. *Jiangsu sheng: Jingkou shanshui zhi*, pp. 24–25.

55. James J. Y. Liu, *The Art of Chinese Poetry* (Chicago: The University of Chicago Press, 1962).

Translation

The Young Bride

He Shuangqing 賀雙卿 was a young woman who lived in Xiaoshan, Jintan. Her family had farmed for generations. She had innate intelligence and she delighted in books. When her maternal uncle was the tutor for the neighborhood boys, she listened to the class recitation in an adjacent room and committed everything to memory. In her teens she exchanged her exceptional embroidery for poetry books and so learned to write poetry herself. Her calligraphy was exquisite; she was able to write the whole of the *Xin jing* 心經 [1] on a cassia leaf. When one of her friends married a scholar, the girl laughed at Shuangqing for not being fated to meet any scholars.

In 1732 Shuangqing was eighteen. Nobody in the mountainous region where she lived knew of her talent. They only praised her for her beauty. That fall she was married to the son of a farm family by the name of Zhou in Xiaoshan, Jintan. The man's mother was once a wet nurse. She and her son rented the land that they farmed and the house where they lived from Zhang Mengzhan 張夢覘. He Shuangqing was very formal toward Landlord Zhang. Her husband was older than she by more than ten years, and except for recognizing a few easy characters in the *Farmers' Almanac*, he is illiterate.

In the fourth month of the summer of 1733 I spent my vacation in Ougeng Studio 耦耕書院 in Xiaoshan (see p. 60). Duan Yuhan 段玉函, also named Huaifangzi 懷芳子, came to visit me. One evening we went out to enjoy the twilight over the hills. We happened to see Shuangqing holding a dust-basket at the entrance of her house. We watched her bring another basket with gourds for planting on the west bank of the bridge. With clear eyes and a fine forehead, her open face nevertheless harbored a trace of sadness.

The following day we obtained a poem of hers written with pollen on a peony leaf, "To the Tune of *Huan xi sha* 浣溪沙":

Warm rain without sentiment, a few dripping strands,
The cowherd holding a branch of flowers at a slant,
It's time for the new wheat
To appear in the small field.
Drawing water from the well to plant melons, I was
Spitefully rebuked for being too early;
Withstanding the smoke in cooking,
I was scolded for taking too much time.
The day is long and pain
Goes through my tender frame.

暖雨無情漏幾絲，牧童斜插嫩花枝，小田新麥上場時。汲水種瓜
偏怒早，忍烟炊黍又嗔遲，日長酸透軟腰肢。

Again she used pollen to write the poem, "To the Tune of *Wang Jiangnan* 望江南" on a tuberose leaf:

Spring, you are nowhere,
I look for you over the rustic bridge in the west.
You're a vision dyed light pink
To trick the butterflies;
You lock your sadness in dark green
To mislead the golden oriole.
My deep sorrow,
Don't bring it up again.

That person, he's nowhere;
Our meeting will be only futile.
When I worship the moon goddess,
Incense stirs my sleeves;
When I mourn the fading of the flowers,
I have no more tears to stain my dress.
The mountain, far away;
The sun, low.

春不見，尋過野橋西。染夢淡紅欺粉蝶，鎖愁濃綠騙黃鸝，幽恨莫重提。　　人不見，相見是還非。拜月有香空惹袖，惜花無淚可沾衣，山遠夕陽低。

Yuhan thought she was making fun of him in her poem. When He Shuangqing heard about this, she said, "Having been born into a mountain family, I know I am not blessed to meet any scholars. Fortunately through the *Sanji* I have made the acquaintance of a few men of talent. Every evening I offer incense and bow to Heaven. I am only a caged bird admiring the high flying phoenix." Then facing the corner of her room, she sighed and said, "Although my husband is ordinary, still he has some regard for me. I don't have the heart to reject him. In this life I don't care to make the acquaintance of scholars." Therefore she wrote the poem, "To the Tune of *Shi luoyi* 濕羅衣":

There's nothing more difficult
To express than hidden sorrow;
Though tears are completely swallowed,
They'll well up again.
I finger the dying flowers;
Speechless, I lean on the screen.
I'm alarmed at my image in the mirror—
I'm sedate and thin,
But my face is not that of spring,
Nor of autumn,
Is it really Shuangqing!

世間難吐只幽情，淚珠嚥盡還生。手撚殘花，無言倚屏，鏡裏相看，自驚瘦亭亭。春容不是，秋容不是，可是雙卿！

Yuhan had a change of heart. He wrote more than ten lyric poems for her and asked for a response, but she made no reply.

One day he happened to see her in front of her door. She looked so haggard and depressed that she did not resemble her former self. Yuhan bowed from afar to say goodbye. He was leaving Xiaoshan and he asked Zhang Mengzhan to find an artist to sketch her likeness for him. He also wrote a farewell poem for her and pleaded for a response. Shuangqing gave him a small envelope carefully sealed with instructions for him to open it on the road when he was alone. Yuhan was elated. Zhang Mengzhan and I knew nothing about this. The next day we sent Zhang Mengzhan's bondmaid to inquire about Shuangqing. The maid reported that Shuangqing only smiled and quoted two lines from Bailuo 白羅 [2] that I had recorded, "Sentiment produces a god of infatuation, / All this only makes the scholar puzzle the more."

An old man in Xiaoshan told me: "Shuangqing does not let convention bind her. She is warm, yet private. With her ambition to soar above the clouds, she is not shy like an ordinary young lady. She does not boast of her talents; visitors never see any trace of her work lying around her home. Her husband is very poor, and her unsympathetic mother-in-law works her hard; yet, she serves them dutifully. Even when she is unhappy, she never appears sullen to her husband. When she is angry, tired, worried or distressed, she still maintains her composure."

Shuangqing's small compound in Xiaoshan was at the foot of the Siping Mountain (四屏山). There were deep bamboo groves where wild flowers grew. There was a colorful bird whose name was unknown but who sang more exquisitely than the golden oriole. On both sides of Shuangqing's compound were huts built by Zhang Mengzhan that he rented out to other tenant farmers. She lived on the west side of the compound. Her door faced an ancient brook, and weeping willows draped over its eaves. When she washed clothes or drew water, she sat gracefully on a rock. Passersby, who caught a glimpse of her in this posture, often mistook her for a fairy. Every time Yuhan came he liked to sit on her rock to enjoy the moonlight on the brook. Outside her court after sunset, one could enjoy the western mountains[3] shrouded by rain, and catch a glimpse of a battered boat abandoned and lodged across the mountain stream. Shuangqing used to sit in that boat to wash her clothes.

Incident of the Frog

On the second day of the fifth month, Zhang Mengzhan and his brother, Renzhi 仁趾, took their servant boy, Ling 齡, for a hike in Siping Mountain. They met a fisherman with a frog in a bamboo cage. It was green, variegated and spotty. It wanted to get out so badly that it was hopping madly about in the cage. They bought it from the fisherman to release it. This they did in the paved area behind their house, where it was shady and grassy. They said a prayer for it in these words:

There will be dew,
So don't bark in the morning;
There will be rain,
So don't cry at night.
You'll drink and eat here,
And as long as you're contented,
You'll be happy.

Zhang Mengzhan wrote a poem for the occasion:

Under the lonely tree west of the bridge
I met a fisherman,
Bought his frog to let roam
East of the winding balustrade.
In the sedge court
Under fine rain and foggy nights,
Cultivate yourself
To become the Toad on the moon.[4]

I responded with these lines:

Squatting on the moss and resting against the grass,
You face this way and that;
Your anger is subsiding,
Since you're out of the fisherman's basket.
If the supernatural carp[5] did not speak up,
He'll still remain in the net.
But don't enjoy the new rain so much
That you'll fuss in the wee hours of the night.

That night Ling heard someone chanting a Buddhist sutra. I told him, "That came from the frog. Once there was a fisherman who caught a boatful of fish. That night he heard the fish chanting sutras. He got so frightened that he threw them back into the sea. Like a clam becoming a Buddha, a mussel becoming a Luohan [a disciple of Buddha], the chant indicates the transition from the end of life's work to release into the blessed land."

This incident became known in the community. Shuangqing responded with a poem, "The Frog" (咏蛙):

Lotus leaves by layers were parted,
Exposing the water to the pavilion.
Hidden fragrance wafted to delight,
Then sired grief in its wake.
The immortal having untied
The ruthless net,
Showers me nightly with gentle rain
From spring to fall.

Reflected by the water, leisurely
I now sit on the grass jetty.
The smartweed is bitter—
I dare not complain of hunger.
Any way to transform myself
Into the toad on the moon?
I only wish to become weightless,
Not to get fat.

蓮葉層開水面樓，暗香生喜便生愁。
仙郎為解無情網，夜雨春恩說到秋。
映水幽閒坐綠磯，蓼辛荼苦敢嫌饑。
何方可化銀蟾去？但願身輕不願肥。

Artist Shilin's Paintings of He Shuangqing

Artist Shilin 石鄰 , formally known as Zhang Fucang 張輔蒼 , came to Xiaoshan and painted two scrolls of Shuangqing planting melons. He asked her to write inscriptions on them. He planned to give one to Yuhan, who commissioned the painting, and keep one for himself.

The last time Yuhan took leave of Xiaoshan, Shuangqing gave him a tiny envelope with the instructions that he was to open it on his way when alone. Yuhan went into a deserted shrine, washed his hands in a brook and licked the seal so that he could open the envelope without tearing it. After the first reading, he became a little vexed, then broke out laughing. Shuangqing had cut a leaf into the shape of a butterfly, and on its two wings she had written two poems, both to the tune of *Huan xi sha*, to make fun of him. This led Yuhan to go to Master Danyuan[6] and ask the latter's friend, Wang Yueqiu 王月虬 , to hire Shilin to come and paint her for him.

On the first day of the sixth month, Shilin said goodbye to Danyuan. It was barely dawn, and Yueqiu, shod in a pair of tall pattens, was waiting for him at the bamboo gate. Shilin greeted him saying, "It's been sunny for a while, why are you in pattens?" Yueqiu smiled and answered, "Just for fun." They picked some pears for breakfast before Shilin started on his journey.

When Shilin arrived at Xiaoshan, he wanted to see Shuangqing immediately, but failed. That evening, Shuangqing was washing clothes under the willows and Shilin was able to observe her on one side; then he moved in front of her to watch. Shuangqing avoided him. Finally Shilin said, "I've got it. Although her bearing is cool, I can still sketch her. The difficulty lies in her hidden grief which at times is apparent and at times is not." After the paintings were finished, he showed them to Shuangqing who inscribed a poem, "Colophon for the Painting 'Planting Melons'," on them. But, after doing this, she regretted her action. Instead, she kept the paintings and refused to return them, thinking the scholars were making fun of her.

For this reason, Mengzhan wrote Shuangqing an erudite letter styled in a defunct form with many allusions. [It is only excerpted here.] Essentially, Zhang Mengzhan explained in his letter to Shuangqing why the painting had been commissioned. He assured her of the scholars' honorable intentions by saying that it was because of their sympathy for, and appreciation of, her talent and beauty that they wanted to spread her fame both in this world among the scholars and the beauties, and in heaven through immortals like Bailuo and Biye,[7] with whom they sometimes communicated through divination. Although Zhang Mengzhan tried to comfort Shuangqing on her ill-fated marriage by saying that she had thus avoided the possibility of being over-shadowed by a scholar spouse, he also wanted her to know that he and his friends were indignant over her suffering and were determined to redirect the intention of Heaven by spreading her good name. Shuangqing was appeased by this and agreed to return the paintings.

Her "Colophon for the Painting 'Planting Melons'" (自題種瓜小影) was written to the tune of *Yujing qiu* 玉京秋. It reads:

> Brow knitted,
> My youthful bloom has faded—
> Much old sorrow I still owe.[8]
> My thin image in the painting,

Inescapable and mortifying!
I'm still drowsy from my new illness—
Even pink rouge
Is a waste of effort.
The cold intensifies during the night;
The bright moon, as if refreshed by a rain,
Is pure, flawless.
On my blue-green sleeves are tear stains;
By their flowery edge
Are countless spots.
No wonder lately
When I comb my hair, bind my feet,
Life, whether salty or sour,[9] is weary for me.
Sweat under my powder brings out the perfume.
I dip my handkerchief into the blue water
To wipe again the bamboo mat.
Who is concerned about me,
A goddess of flowers
Exiled temporarily on earth?

眉半斂，春紅已全褪，舊愁還欠。畫中瘦影，羞人難閃。新病三分未醒，淡胭脂，空費輕染。涼生夜，月華如洗，素娥無玷。翠袖啼痕堪驗，海棠邊，曾沾萬點。怪近來，尋常梳裹，酸鹹都厭。粉汗凝香，蘸碧水，羅帕時揩冰簟。有誰念？原是花神暫貶。

Shilin, on reading her poem, sighed. Then he said, "In this intense heat I am dizzy in both my eyes and my heart. I had to crouch in the chestnut grove just to sketch her." So he departed. Zhang Mengzhan wrote a poem for him as a parting gift.[10]

Studio in the Mountain

Zhang Mengzhan's compound at Xiaoshan included on its west side an irregular shaped room named Gudian shanfang 古電山房

(Ancient Lightning Mountain Studio). It featured on the wall a couplet written by Anshu:[11]

> My heart is in the state of being released from waking;
> My feelings are in the mood of waiting for a dream to return.

There was also a poem by Danyuan:

> Shouldering the pick homeward, I enjoy
> The neglected flowers coming through the cracks of the bamboo fence.
> Toward evening summer clouds take on remarkable forms;
> A golden blue-green haze defuses the mulberry grove.
>
> This helps to broaden my feelings,
> Fusing my heart with what I see.
> Need I wait till my farm work is done?
> The mere acceptance of what I see is leisure gained.
>
> During the quiet evening a bird may suddenly cry out;
> Through the bamboo the moonlight spills.
> Often I put out the candle on my desk
> To enjoy this leisure into the middle of the night.

Furnishings consisted of a bamboo divan, two stone tables, one big and one small, a stone stove and a stone wash basin in which there were some duckweed and tiny bream. The mountain people presented Mengzhan with an old cedar root that can be used for sitting or reclining. In one corner of the compound was a huge tree, harboring large cicadas that chirp shrilly and long. In the summer toward noon, the shade from the tree moved over to the windows of the court, and the soft breeze drifted in. One could lie on the bamboo divan or settle at the stone table. The farmers' singing rose here and there from the mist at the foot of the mountain, and it was moving, especially when you were mindful of their hard life.

Among the rocks luxuriant grass grew. The drier the earth, the denser the grass. The mountain children had turned a praying mantis loose in the grass. When it eyed a small insect for a kill, how it cocked its head, extended an angry arm, bent its belly and lifted its foot! I had painted it in watercolor and at times was able to catch its delightful movements. The children had also caught crickets and hidden them near the head of the divan. Gather up the curtains and the setting moon spilled over half the wall, bringing in the cool autumn air from the eaves.

One day I sat on the old cedar root and told the servant boy, Ling, about the ten continents and the three islands. Renzhi was burning pine branches at the stone stove to brew tea. Mengzhan chimed in to say, "On the peak of Kunlun 崑崙 there is a bronze column with a circumference of 3,000 *li*. It penetrates the sky, and so one could carve steps into it and walk right up into heaven." Renzhi suggested that the easier way to reach heaven is to walk up the steps of the nine tiers of Xumi Mountain (須彌山), which he said is on the northwest of Kunlun and only 3,360,000 *li* high.

While we were having fun bantering, Shuangqing sent back through Mengzhan's bondmaid the paintings of her planting melons. She had cut out her inscriptions on the paintings before returning them. At that moment Mengzhan happened to be playing with the praying mantis on his fan. He was relaxed, leaning on the stone table. But he became so irritated by what Shuangqing had done to the paintings that he threw down the insect and cried out, "But this is tipping heaven toward the northwest! We must demand that Shuangqing cultivate the five-color stones to mend the sky!"[12]

North of Xiaoshan there was a huge rock that stands erect like a screen forty to fifty feet tall and half again as wide. There were old cypress, cedar, and pine trees growing in distorted forms, hugging the ground or hunchbacked, all bound by ancient vines. Under the precipice it was sunless. There was a thatched pavilion facing north with a name plaque of "Xiang xia" 響霞 (Resounding

Sunset's Glow). Danyuan once wrote a poem about it. A meandering brook came through the rambling rocks, keeping the stones awash. In the front the water converged and gathered into a pond about four feet deep. At the shallow portion where there were pebbles, you could wade across. In the middle of the pond a stone jutted out like the spine of an ox, complete with shoulders and a head. Hollow underneath, it harbored some fish that were very delicious. About a hundred paces from the west of the pavilion, a studio had been built, wrapping around the precipice. It faced east and was named Ougeng 耦耕 (Farming in Pairs). Bamboo, well trimmed, surrounded it. Toward the north was Chonggang 重岡 Peak; ten *li* further north was Mao Shan 茅山 . From the upper story of this studio you could actually see the steps leading to the mountain top.

Mengzhan's studio, Gudian shanfang, was located at the southwest edge of Xiaoshan. The route from the western foot of the hill to Xiang xia Pavilion was about 500 paces, running through a bamboo forest with huge rocks on both sides. There were eight turns and five ups and downs. Ougeng Studio featured a poem on a screen written by Yin Xiacun 殷霞村 [13] about the bamboo:

> Half a court of moss dotted in thick ink,
> Impassively I view Langgan 琅玕 Peak, I don't care to go home.
> You laugh at the crushing snow not because you are jointless;
> You desire to soar above the clouds, don't doubt yourself.
> Where your leaves are thin you let in the sunlight;
> When one stays too long in your depth, the cool prevails.
> I especially enjoy viewing you through the night window after
>   the lamp is blown,
> As you quietly move the shadow of the moon nearer to my teacup.
> Your rhythm is brought out in your hovering over the studio;
> In the moonlight your blue-green leaves drip with dew.
> Without earthiness you need no dusting;
> At times you may look sad but you always recover.

The soil you're in is poor, cool as the gentleman is quiet;
When it gets cold you slant your branches like a lady swaying.
Your grace and virtue are worthy of an ode,
Let the immortal scholar do you the homage of these few lines.

On the left was a small studio named Qiuyou 求友 (In Search of Friendship). Its wall featured one of Anshu's four-character poems in three stanzas:

Rain, rain everyday,
Profusely watering the flowers, bamboos,
Prolonging the glow of the sunset,
Lashing the mountain's emerald green.
The gentleman enjoys his thoughts.
Being fed grains grown by Heaven.

Rain, rain everyday,
Indulging the flowers and bamboos.
There's a bird with friendly sounds—
I'm not alone in making poetry.
I look forward to its coming—
The shepherd of the sunset's glow.

Rain, rain everyday,
The leafy shade gets thicker,
The daily rain thins flowers.
Subtle light glistening and wet
Awaits me at the rustic gate.
Vanishing are shadows and flowers.

These poems in both the Gudian shanfang and Qiuyou studios were written in the calligraphy of Chen Zainan 陳載南 , also named Xingye 星野 ;[14] they bestowed a feeling of tranquility.

Behind the compound there was an earthen hill encrusted with rocks and stones. It bore no name but was distinguished by a cave called "Rouge Cave." The peach-colored powder milled from the stones of this hill, when mixed with cosmetic powder, was used by the ladies for freckles. Above the cave there was a rocky cliff, on top of which was an ancient temple erected for a graceful idol in the form of a beautiful lady. The mountain people called it the Temple of the Goddess of Flowers. Anshu has written a poem about it.

One time when the hillside was in flowers, Mengzhan and I climbed up the cliff to sacrifice to this goddess. All we did was to drip some wine and burn some poetry for her. It was midsummer then, yet in the mountain the evening was like autumn, the forest was dark and deep with mystery. We did not hear human voices, only strange pecking and whistling. Wild fires started at times. If we could not bear this kind of primeval feeling, we would run off. When evening came and we were relaxing after reading aloud, we might concentrate in order to hear the running brook. We tied extra thin broken tiles, dozens of them, under the eaves of the temple and in the bamboo grove. When they hit one another, they made pleasant sounds. During windy or rainy evenings, they struck with crispness. For this reason we called them blue-green bells. Mengzhan has tried to write a poem about them but up to now has not succeeded. When he gets it done, he wants to send it to Danyuan, Xiacun and Anshu for their harmonization.

On Friendship

Anshu's view on friendship was as follows:

> If you know what kind of people to avoid, you would know the kind of people you should get to know. What kind of people are to be avoided? Those who deprecate others; those who never talk of the good but only of the bad of others; those who dwell on grudges; those who are suspicious of others' speech and action; those who cannot differentiate between right and wrong, good and bad; those who are

embarassed by their own poverty; those who fish for a name; those who look humble on the outside but are haughty inside; those who do not accept sincere admonition; those who serve coarse food at home but criticize the food served by others; those who don't appreciate the labor of farmers; those who are over-superstitious—all these people are to be avoided in friendship.

Yu Quhu 于屈湖, son of Master Yu Nanshe 于南社, who teaches in Lishui 溧水, is a good friend of Xiao Songshan 蕭松山. One day they went out of the city gate to sit in the Huaibai Pavilion (懷白亭). Songshan said, "Today people form many undesirable friendships. A person could fool you by his false attitude, superficial name, put-on elegance, overdone respectfulness. The principle of friendship is derived from the human relationship of brotherly love where one extends to friends aid-in-kind, as well as helping them become upright. One does not acquiesce to the bad conduct of a friend; he does not talk of a friend behind his back; he does not retract a promise or change with the weather toward a friend. In the *Li ji* 禮記 (Book of Rites),[15] it is said, 'Be united in your direction and aspiration, apply the same means for the same end; when you stand together, you will rejoice, you will not get tired of each other.' If you have not seen a friend for some time, don't believe in rumors about him. Let us take an oath to this kind of friendship."

Quhu wrote this down and sent it to me for my *Sanji*. I think Songshan's view on friendship really gets to the root of the matter.

I recall when I sent Mengzhan off to his autumn examination in 1732, we passed by Lishui and wanted to visit Songshan. Quhu told us, "When you come back this way, I shall buy some thousand-day mountain wine and drink with you in Huaibai Pavilion, so that together with Songshan, we may enjoy the ancient cypress, let the pine scent waft their music into our ears, and wash our caps in the brook under the moonlight. Why don't we wait until then?"

After this I engaged a carriage to go up to the ledge of a

precipice of Mao Shan before we returned. There I became emotional about my future and regretted that I did not take an oath of friendship with Quhu. At that time I did not know Songshan well. After I heard Songshan's views on friendship, I felt even more desolate. I regret that I have not yet the opportunity to shake his hand. I bring out Anshu's words to compare them with his. I admire Quhu's great knowledge and heroic air, the way he could find real friendship in the empty mountains and the flowing streams [making friends with hermits]. In the mountain of Lishui there is a spring the water of which transforms one into an immortal. It is called Fenghuang quan 鳳凰泉 (Phoenix Spring). Songshan's words are water from that spring.

The Scholar Schoolmates

I studied in the western mountains for over two years. To enrich my classical studies I made use of the evening mist and the sunset's glow to write poetry and lyrics. [Note: As a cousin[16] of Mengzhan and Renzhi's, Shi Zhenlin was invited to study with them by their father, Master Xiuyuan, who tutored them.]

Mengzhan, aged twenty-five, and his brother Renzhi, twenty-four, are not interested in power or profit, they do not care for famous names or riches. Their father, Master Xiuyuan stayed home to teach them and for this reason discouraged friends from visiting. My late friend, Xu Yiyu 許逸輿,[17] advised him that I am not the type to be caged and imprisoned. Therefore, Master Xiuyuan expanded his tutorage to take in more boarding students. This was how Yuhan 玉函, Xingye 星野, Yungu 雲古, Danyuan 澹圓, Xiacun 霞村, Fengqi 鳳岐 and Anshu 闇叔 all came to the school.

These gentlemen have no desire to associate with the rich. At leisure they go bareheaded and barefooted. They are self-reliant individuals and free in their speech. Their lofty ideals can persuade even those who admire officialdom to change their minds. Having been nurtured in their midst, the brothers, Mengzhan and Renzhi, have learned a great deal from their discussions and writings. They have acquired a feeling of expansive competence; they declare that they now have a new perspective on life and above all, appreciate friends with high ideals. They believe that outside the classics, there are many things bestowed on men by the gods. Their father, Master Xiuyuan, is getting old, and the two of them have been given their individual quarters and their inheritance for them to set up their own households for their families. I myself am preparing to go off on a journey in search of extraordinary people. I do not want to bury my head in a desk and live a meaningless life.

Joy of Farming

There are experiences in one's life which may be incidental but unforgettable; they cannot be repeated even if one wished it. These are things I can talk about with feeling.

When I was three or four, I loved hedgehogs. Hedgehogs have quills like the burrs of a chestnut. When a hedgehog sees people, it rolls itself up into a ball. Whenever I had a crying spell, nothing could stop my crying except the sight of a hedgehog, for it made me laugh. I used to kick it to make it roll. I also had two mother rabbits that I took to bed with me, cradling them in my arms. I fed them bean leaves but they refused to eat and died. I cried over them for several days.

When I was eight or nine, I took a basket and went to pick cotton. Bringing along some grilled biscuits, I asked a neighborhood boy by the name of Brother Zhong, who was a year older than I, to accompany me. We sat in the cotton patch and enjoyed the biscuits together. Among the cotton was planted sesame on which we found some green caterpillars larger than silkworms. I squeezed these worms to scare my companion. He pretended to be afraid, knitting his brow and cringing to make me laugh. In later years, even after I had grown up, I still liked to pick cotton. Cotton should be picked when the weather is cloudy. If you pick it under a hot sun, the leaves will crumble and adhere to the flowers. During a good day it is best to start picking while the dew is still on the plant and to stop working at noon. Sometimes I picked both the cotton and the beans that are usually planted with it, and then separated them when I got home.

When I was young though, I did not really enjoy the fun involved. Two years ago when I returned home to Lake Tao (洮湖) from the western mountains, I took my young son to pick cotton north of the village. It was a cool day in late autumn, the millet and the corn were luxuriant and golden. The early rice had been harvested, the late vegetables were just coming up. Around the fields only the distant peaks were green. White feathery clouds drifted throughout the sky; dragonflies were darting about, and insects buzzing. The flat fields, the long hills, the lonely tree, the abandoned nests, the farmers at different chores with their hoes and scythes, pressing on, backing up, bending or lifting—when I saw them, I admired them for working so naturally and contentedly. My young son became thirsty, I found a leftover melon among the abandoned vines. It was as large as a fist and very sweet. Locusts flew past with clicking wings. My son caught one, which I had him release soon afterwards. We came home rather late. We took our time chattering as we sauntered home. At a distance from our house I could see that under the shade of the mulberry and date trees, the late afternoon sun filled the entrance of the house; my aged mother was leaning on the door, waiting for our return.

He Shuangqing and Anshu

On the fifteenth day of the eighth month I dreamed that Yuhan was in Mengzhan's studio and that Anshu came in afterwards. I dreamed that they were reading the poem "Peony" aloud.

Before this, Mengzhan had wanted to visit Anshu in the fall and to go boating with him on East Lake but had hesitated because he felt that the trip might be too far. When he heard about my dream, he said, "How will Anshu come, since he is always sick? If it is by land, he dislikes sedan chairs; if by water, he dislikes boats. There's simply no way to persuade him to come."

On the evening of the sixteenth day, we were taken by surprise when Yuhan knocked at the door to tell us that he and Anshu had just arrived. By the time Mengzhan got out of bed and found his slippers, Anshu was already entering the western compound of Langgan (琅玕西院). There was no time to bring in candles and so we greeted each other under the moonlight. Anshu saluted with his hands folded saying, "Now I've come because of Mengzhan. Our boat traveled two hundred *li* in one day. I tapped on the rail to beat time and sang Shuangqing's poetry. All of a sudden Heaven sent the wind and so we literally flew!"

Since it was already midnight, they returned to their boat for the night. The moon was bright and the dew heavy. Walking back and forth on the river embankment, Anshu was eager to know where Shuangqing lived. Early the next morning he went to the Ougeng Studio to enjoy the scenery. He hiked up the mountain and squatted on a rock. He relished Juqu 句曲 , Fangtai 方台 and Ji Mountains (髻山) to the west; he pointed to Lakes Tao and Dafu 大涪 in the east; he viewed the peaks of Tongguan 銅官 , Langgan 琅玕, Xianren 仙人 and Qiaoshi 巧石 to the south; he inquired about Mount Heng (横山), Hezhu 鶴渚 and Lake Si (思湖) in the north. He was so impressed by what he saw that he held

Mengzhan's hand and solemnly declared, "Colorful precipices and magnificent billows, exquisite flora and fauna, cool and sublime—they go on without end. No wonder this place produces a beauty unprecedented and unique!"

Shuangqing at that time was recovering from her illness. She had to draw water from the well, cook and bring lunch to the field. Overworking during her recuperation soon brought on the malaria again. With no appetite, she subsisted on a few bowls of thin rice porridge each day. Her mother-in-law and her husband scolded her relentlessly for being lazy, so she forced herself to stay up. She cooked and would sit at the stove, for she was not supposed to go beyond the threshold. Anshu came to the front of her door and loudly recited her poetry. Dressed in white silk and fanning himself with a feather fan, he sat on a reclining willow to sing and whistle shrilly. Then lost in his agony, he made distressing sounds. Still, Shuangqing could not be persuaded to come out to meet him.

Anshu wrote a poem for Shuangqing, which reads:

> Pity yourself for being so thin
> As to fear the weight of your chiffon;
> The lamp dims its shadow
> In affinity with your illness.
> When you doze off,
> Are you aware it may be goodbye?
> The autumn rain chills your dream
> But begs indulgence for the sound it makes.

Yuhan wrote a lyric to the tune of *Zhuying yaohong* 燭影搖紅 for her:

> Deep green is the shade of the willow;
> She remains in the spring mist far away.
> Since we parted at the end of the earth, I've written;

Recalling the past, I'm overwhelmed.
Re-examining closely your poem on an old leaf,
I'm afraid the fragrance of the pollen and the flower will
evaporate.
Your tiny writing—
It is there, though difficult to read—
Brings up mingling sadness.

A dream without ending;
My tears will add to the water at the front gate.
The green hills face each other, the sun is low.
I see your image and I shed tears.
Alone, in the bottom of my heart
I'm forever wondering how you've been lately.
Who appreciates talent?
Reciting your beautiful poetry over and over again,
I shall remember it in my next life.

Shuangqing rolled up these poems and inserted them into her sleeve without saying anything. Toward sunset she came out to wash clothes. Her hair was wrapped in fine silk, she looked frail. Anshu held onto the branch of a willow tree and recited her poetry. After finishing her wash, she calmly turned toward home with her head bowed and closed the door behind her. She never lifted her head to glance at him.

On the twentieth day Mengzhan's bondmaid brought over two poems from Shuangqing, one written on an impatien leaf, and the other on a trumpet flower leaf. The writing was so small it was hardly legible. The poems were:

Lightly Sketched (淡寫)

Lightly I sketch the chilled blooms,
Pray to the supreme diety.
The blue clouds have blown in

Some heart-breaking frost.
Signs of tender sadness
Are imprinted on the golden millet—
Throughout the night the goddess of flowers[18]
Must have been busy gathering the fallen petals.

淡寫涼紅叩玉皇，碧雲吹下斷腸霜。
嫩愁細印黃金粟，一夜花神又費忙。

Resunning Garments（更曬）

To air again the autumn garments
I use the evening sun.
The beautiful mountain can ease somewhat
My sickly countenance.
If only my spirit could leave my body
To become a firefly among the weeds,
My inner grievance would emerge like ice
And turn into pure crystal!

After the swallows the wild geese
Fly in and out of formation;
By the rainpool the shattered moon
Is coming back to life.
Through the small window the glow
Of the night sky is usually dim,
I'll use it as a lamp,
Sit up till dawn.

更曬秋衣就晚晴，好山能照病容清。
離魂附草爲螢火，幽恨如冰化水晶。
燕後新鴻連復斷，雨邊殘月死還生。
小窗夜色從來淡，便爲燈花坐到明。

Since Anshu's arrival on the sixteenth, he had seen Shuangqing three times, two times from the side and once from the front. He must have walked back and forth in front of her door more than ten thousand paces and recited her poetry a thousand times. When Shuangqing heard about this, she said, "Anshu must be the most heart-broken person of all time!" One day Anshu spread some dry grass under a willow tree near her house, sat on the grass and recited her poetry. Shuangqing had come home after picking cotton, and her mother-in-law happened to have locked the gate and gone out. Anshu was leaning with his back on the door to watch. He saw Shuangqing far away in the shade of the willow, raising her sleeves a few times as if wiping tears.

When he returned to Mengzhan's he threw himself onto the bed and covered his head with a quilt. His old heart trouble had recurred. He was given some herbs, rhizomes of goldthread and the raw roots of *Rehmannia lutea*, to chew and that eased the pain. On the twenty-second day he engaged a boat to go east. Shuangqing sent him a poem to chide him containing the line: "In the eighth month the howling wind stirs the willow catkins."

I took this occasion to tell Anshu, "Shuangqing is beautiful and talented, she is also a dutiful wife—she does not want to hurt her husband. There was someone who laughed at her husband for being an illiterate. Restraining her anger, Shuangqing commented, 'Literates are only fit for watching pickle jars[19] and taking care of children!' " Anshu said, "Alas, Shuangqing must be an itinerant fairy!" He took his time walking to the boat. Shuangqing happened to be washing clothes on the other side of the woods and so he did not see her before he left.

We went together on the boat to visit Danyuan. The next day, joined by Yu Shushan 于墅山, we went to Dongguo 東郭 to look for the artist Shilin, for Anshu wanted him to paint Shuangqing for him. We did not find Shilin home and therefore left. When we got to the Wuli Pavilion (五里亭), Anshu reminded me to comfort Shuangqing with these words, "Please tell her not to let her fate drown her in self-pity. In the tenth month I am going to pick some hibiscus to offer to her portrait. I shall pray to the Buddha to forgive all the weaker sex from their trespasses. I shall paint three thousand portraits of her to give to people who appreciate her."

On the twenty-third day of the eighth month Anshu left Wuli Pavilion to walk back to East Lake. Yuhan and I stayed at the Nanchan Shrine (南禪寺). As we sat under a lamp, Yu Shushan asked me to tell him about Shuangqing. After this, he wrote three poems with the intention of sending them to her. Danyuan who was with us, sat on the meditation divan facing south. He expounded on the Dao and talked of decorum with the idea of disparaging Shuangqing. Yuhan disliked Danyuan's punctiliousness; he did not want to listen to him and so went to lie down. I said to Danyuan, "You know, when Shuangqing got hold of a collection of your poetry, she washed her hands before she held it, rinsed her mouth before she read it. She admires you so much that she vows she will carve your likeness to pay her respects to you. Alas, she does not know how badly you think of her!" Immediately Danyuan stood up, raised his eyebrows and hands and asked me, "Really?" I told him I do not lie. He apologized and said, "My poetry is not easily understood by many men, and now I have a lady who understands me. I should know better. Here I am so much older than she. I would be ashamed to face her now." From that time on he did not dare moralize over Shuangqing. Yuhan was elated by this incident.

Weicheng 薇城 , the younger brother of Feng Maocun 馮茅村 , painted and wrote poetry. He was very sensitive. He appeared cold but was actually warm-hearted. He empathized with the unfortunate. Once he read some of Shuangqing's poetry. Immediately he changed color and fell silent. He held onto her poems to read and reread them and did not utter a word for the rest of the day.

I saw Yuhan off, picked some flowers for him from the roadside, and told him, "From now on we have an added dimension to our sadness."

Harvest Time: More Paintings of the Poet and Her Further Bouts with Malaria

It was the ninth month and Shuangqing's malaria was still unabated. She assisted occasionally in the rice harvest, and would force herself to work in the threshing yard. After picking up the stiff, damp stalks of grain, hulling and winnowing, then drying and storing them, she grew tired and dizzy. She would sit down on the grass to rest, but no sooner was she settled than she would be up again. The neighborhood women pleaded with her to stop. She wept and said, "My husband left early this morning with a sickle. He went barefoot in the frost, suffering lesions all over his feet and toes. When he works so hard in the field, how can I sit and watch? My mother-in-law is old, still she works in the field. An ill-fated person like myself, how can I act like a rich girl, to be afraid of the wind and the sun, and hide from dust and sand?" The neighborhood women all grieved for her.

Shuangqing would wear a peasant's dress with her clean white sleeves rolled up. Once as she swept the threshing yard, a piece of paper fell from her sleeve and was picked up by the servant boy Ling. It read: "The lamp dims its shadow / In affinity with your illness." [This is from Anshu's poem to Shuangqing, see p. 68.] She was sickly and went about in a daze. Every time she was outside, she would bow her head, lower her eyes and would not look around. One time she happened to carry some vegetables over the West Bridge; she put the basket under the willow and began to plait two branches into a knot, smiled and said, "This is a benevolent tree."

On the ninth day of that month, Shilin came. Shilin was very poor. He was devoted to painting and wrote poetry all the time, even when traveling. This time he painted three scrolls of Shuangqing: one of her gazing at the moon, one of her carrying lunch to the field, and the third of her washing clothes at the brook. Mengzhan had the portraits brought to her with two gifts, a brass hairpin and two bolts [60 Chinese feet each] of moon-blue, wispy, light cotton,[20] and asked her to write inscriptions on the paintings.

Shuangqing was in the midst of the harvest; she was worn out by the labor. Her poor hands were blistered, her fingers calloused, and there were traces of blood on her limbs. She stretched out her arms to show Mengzhan's bondmaid, saying, "With all this how can I still hold a brush and write?" Shilin and I had picked some wild chrysanthemums and were going around the orchard, when we spotted her in the field wearing a thin white jacket. She was leaning against the threshing bed, gathering the grain and the tares. Straw was sticking onto her chignon and scattered all over her shoulders. When Shilin left on the twenty-fourth day, we saw him part way up the dike. Mengzhan recited one of Anshu's poems for him and we watched until he disappeared before we turned back. On our way home we saw Shuangqing wearing several layers of quilted jackets. She was sunning unhusked rice at the western wall. Actually it was very warm, but she looked cold. We knew that she was having a bout with malaria.

The weather remained beautiful until the end of the month. Farmers were busy bringing in the harvest. Their harvested grain filled the ditches between the fields and orchards. Grain was piled up everywhere, like little hills. The women worked outside from morning till night. Shuangqing's malaria worsened. Her fever gave her dizzy spells, and her face became exceedingly yellow. However, her mother-in-law pressured her without mercy, scolding loudly if Shuangqing was but a trifle slow. After lunch Shuangqing's intermittent fever made her so cold that she trembled. But she forced herself to stay out, putting on layers of quilted clothing. When she carried the grain basket, you could see every grain in it trembling. When she was feverish, she wore only a single layer of clothing; her face turned crimson, and her breathing became difficult. When she got thirsty, and there was no boiled water, she simply went to the river for a drink.

Now and then her mother-in-law would glance at her sideways and abuse her with cold words. Shuangqing never answered back. Rather, she kept a smile on her face and was solicitous at every turn. She tried to be the first to get to a job, for she was afraid to burden her mother-in-law. She helped her scatter straw on the field; while the old woman spread ten handfuls, she had already spread a hundred. Her every movement was full of grace. Her eyebrows were thin as if drawn with a brush, her earrings sparkled like stars. When she turned up her sleeves to wipe her sweat, her countenance was radiant. Always suspicious, her mother-in-law never allowed any man within talking distance of Shuangqing. On the other hand, Shuangqing was also careful; when you spoke to her, she never answered you.

At the beginning of the ninth month Anshu sent her a letter which read:

> I came to pay you a visit and read your poetry. I have found you are exquisite, without peer in heaven or on earth. For this reason I am overjoyed. I cannot imagine how that must have made me behave. You admonished me for doing violence to the willow catkins; I shall take heed.
>
> I appreciate talent, something I have been searching for all these years without much success. When I finally met Shi Zhenlin, I was satisfied and dared not look further, because I know talent is the most difficult thing to find. How could I ever have dreamed of meeting you? My meeting you is the most fortunate thing that has happened to me; your meeting Shi Zhenlin is the most fortunate thing to happen in your unfortunate life.
>
> What will be handed down? There's no worry that your name will not go down in history, but a name can also be the cause of slander. You must not belittle your own writing and waste it on false admirers.

One evening Shuangqing worked alone in the threshing yard after her family had quit and gone to their baths. The moon was in the clouds and a wind arose. Here and there dogs began to whimper. She sat on the hay to bundle the straw, then piled the bundles together. The servant boy Ling came up behind her and startled her with a sudden noise. Shuangqing was frightened and that made her malaria grow worse.

At first Anshu thought the worsening of Shuangqing's malaria was due to some phantom plaguing her. Playfully he wrote a poem and drew a charm for the phantom's exorcism. After this incident, Shuangqing laughingly asked Ling, "Will the charm painter be coming again?" She loved chrysanthemums. She planted some in broken crocks and placed them where she could see them when she cooked. Her poem "The Chrysanthemum" (菊花) written to the tune of *Erlang shen* 二郎神 reads:

The frail willow, like silk,
Gracefully breaks up the light mist as usual
Into shadows on the autumn hill at sunset.
I'm glad your flowering branches
Have not withered.
You've endured bitter rain through Chongyang,[21]
Now made the tenth month.
I know tonight
There'll be a touch of frost;
By the time butterflies leave,
You'll naturally lower your head.

Intensely
You are suffering in your bones
Pain from the season's first chill.
Unfortunately I'll have to be ungracious,
To desert you when evening's quiet comes.
With the moon so cold over the railing,
I cannot sleep;

For many nights I've stayed up
Without letting down the bed curtains.
In vain you bloom for a poor family;
There's no wine for you to dispel your sorrow.

絲絲脆柳，裊破淡烟依舊。向落日，秋山影裏，還喜花枝未瘦。苦雨重陽挨過了，虧耐到小春時候。知今夜，蘸微霜，蝶去自垂首。　　生受，新寒浸骨，病來還又。可是我雙卿薄倖，撇你黃昏靜後。月冷闌干人不寐，鎮幾夜未鬆金扣，枉孤卻，開向貧家，愁處欲澆無酒。

One day Shuangqing was late bringing lunch to her husband in the fields. He got so angry that he swung his hoe at her. When she turned homeward, she wrote this poem to the tune of *Ji gu luan* 寄孤鸞:

As luck would have it, the midday freeze
Began when my intermittent fever was coming on.
I put on an extra blue jacket;
My chignon being dishevelled from sleep,
Carelessly I tied a scarf to keep my hair in place.
In my haste I neglected to wash my plain skirt;
On its folding seam
Are a couple of silk threads broken.
A close look at my wrists shows they're calloused;
Still, my cheeks are youthful.
At least I've survived all the miseries in life,
Even though I may be reduced to ashes.
At the time of marriage
I had dreams of happiness—
Guess they've turned to smoke in the kitchen.
At the eastern fallow field there were rebukes for lunch was late;
Tides of chill overcome me—
My fever, who is concerned?
Must dash home to retrieve the cotton being sunned;
Very soon dinner needs to be tended to again.

午寒偏準，早瘧意初來。碧衫添襯，宿髻慵梳，亂裹帕羅齊鬢。忙中素裙未浣，摺痕邊，斷絲雙損。玉腕近看如繭，可香腮還嫩。

算一生淒楚也拚忍，便化粉成灰。嫁時先忖，錦思花情，敢被爨烟薰盡。東菑卻嫌餉緩，冷潮回，熱潮誰問？歸去將棉曬取，又晚炊相近。

At the end of another day she was coming from the threshing yard with a broom and a dust-basket in her hands, when she spotted a lonely wild goose crying pitifully as it came to rest on an embankment. While she stood watching it, her mother-in-law came to her without warning from the back and reprimanded her for pausing. Startled, she dropped her basket. Being by temperament easily scared and nervous, she was further reduced by her long illness to a nervous wreck. Her mother-in-law knew this; that was the reason she did such a terrible thing to Shuangqing. In spite of this incident Shuangqing wrote a poem on the lonely wild goose (孤雁) to the tune of *Xi huanghua man* 惜黃花慢:

Azure over the distant sky
Except for scattered,
Red fragments of the sunset.
When I listen, I dread seeing you close by;
When I look, I fear you are far away.
Lonely wild goose,
To whose side are you heading?
The white frost is already caking the rush bank;
Don't dally,
Or be envious of the loving seagulls—
Go to sleep quietly by yourself.
To be of a phoenix pair is splendid;
After all, their marriage is made in heaven.

With grief I implore you not to complain;
Make use of the sandbar, little pond,
Pass your fleeting days for the time being.

Your chance at the grain is gone,
Nets are stretched everywhere to get you;
Even in dreams your spirit will be disturbed.
Cold smoke rises from only a few houses.
Your grief for your mate
In your little heart
Must be inextricable!
The night is not yet over;
Tired, you may lose your chance of alighting
Except in an open field.

碧盡遙天，但暮霞散綺，碎剪紅鮮。聽時愁近，望時怕遠。孤鴻一個，去向誰邊？素霜已冷蘆花渚，更休倩，鷗鷺相憐，暗自眠。鳳凰縱好，寧是姻緣。　　淒涼勸你無言，趁一沙半水，且度流年。稻粱初盡，網羅正苦，夢魂易驚。幾處寒烟。斷腸可似嬋娟意，寸心裏，多少纏綿！夜未闌，倦飛誤宿平田。

Chen Xigu 陳希古 was a young man who had just returned from the prosperous province of Zhejiang 浙江 . He was handsome and rich but snobbish. He claimed to be a cousin of Shuangqing. He brought her some poems, imitating the ancient style, but unreadable, along with gifts of handkerchiefs, towels, earrings and silk. Shuangqing's husband, a hunch-back, served him food, but Chen put on an arrogant air toward his host and even made fun of him. This irritated Shuangqing. She wept and refused his gifts. On the back of his poems she wrote:

This poetry is only an imitation of the genuine and is given to impress me. Cloth and grain are not rare; even children know they are wholesome, and they are found in the ordinary homes of us mountain folk. Yet, are they not superior to the first fire sticks discovered by Suiren 燧人 [22] and the first mortar and pestle for herbal medicine invented by Shennong 神農 ?[23] There are stele monuments of the Qin dynasty and commemorative pillars of the Han dynasty, books and sutras from the immortals and the gods, but how many people ever touch these

> things? They will never take the place of spontaneous songs and laments. The writer of these poems is trying to fool himself by making a storm in a teapot.

Chen felt humiliated. He came to me to complain about Shuangqing, cursing her saying, "An ill-fated person! She certainly makes me mad!" Mengzhan placated him and sent him away.

My Trip to Visit Scholar Friends

[I], the Young Immortal Who Plays with the Moon [i.e., Shi himself], put on my coarse tunic and grass sandals, followed the woodcutter into the mountain and got myself tangled in brambles and bruised by rocks and gravel. My tunic was torn and my sandals ruined, exposing my elbows and heels. Some well-dressed people made fun of my appearance; I in turn enjoyed laughing with them. When they asked me to change my clothes and sandals, I would not answer them.

In 1733 on the fifteenth day of the tenth month, I planned to visit Yun Ningxi 惲寧溪, Chao Nazhai 巢納齋 and Zheng Chi'an 鄭癡菴 at Menghe 孟河. To equip me for my travel, Mengzhan brought me some clothes, Renzhi gave me a hat, and the servant boy Ling brought me a pair of shoes. I thanked them and took leave of their chrysanthemums. Then I engaged a boat, taking Master Danyuan along. I carried in my luggage my *Sanji* manuscript and the painting of Shuangqing washing clothes. After spending twenty days away, I returned one evening to Mengzhan's Danxiang Hall (澹香堂). My immediate greeting was to ask about the chrysanthemums. I might have looked a little dilapidated but was still neat and tidy.

Mengzhan asked how Chi'an was doing and what he had thought of the *Sanji* and the painting of Shuangqing. I told him:

Chi'an has a good physique, and he always speaks well of people. His home is elegant and spacious, full of books and plants. On the wall are two ancient *qin* zithers, three undecorated flutes, and one drum. The zithers are for himself, the flutes are for Ningxi. He has lined up fifteen kinds of chrysanthemums as a screen, and above these flowers he hung Shuangqing's painting. He brought out an antique tripod for incense. Sitting on one side, he began to drum out a mournful *cao* 操 [24] to honor Shuangqing. He wanted to play the tune of Shuangqing's lyric, *Xi huanghua man* (Lonely Wild Goose) on his zither. He declared: "If good-hearted people won't sing Shuangqing's poetry and play a *cao* for her, I would not shine on them if I were the moon; I wouldn't breathe on them if I were the wind." He often mentioned Anshu and referred to Cao Zhenting 曹震亭 [another scholar friend] as an admirable person. Many times he raised his hands to salute you. When we were leaving, he took his zither and walked with us for twenty *li* so that he could play it for us before parting.

Mengzhan asked about Nazhai 納齋 . I told him:

Nazhai has a fine beard. He is trustworthy, not proud and never makes flowery remarks. You don't have to know him to sense he's a kindly person. Danyuan and I arrived at Chi'an's on the third day of the month. That evening it thundered and rained, but Chi'an sent his servant boy to fetch Nazhai from Gucun 固村 . Next day the two came with several layers of their clothing soaked. Nazhai said, "Yesterday I was somewhere else, and so I missed a whole day's fun." I looked at him, sighed and said, "You look pale, unlike five years ago when I last saw you. Fortunately, your beard is more beautiful, without a touch of white. Your father must be about eighty-five. Is he well? People always say that you take good care of your parents. In contrast, I don't do as well for my mother."

I asked to see some of his writing. He showed me ten or more pieces, all of which are on filial piety and chivalry. There is nothing in a lighter vein. His poetry is calm, warm and honest. Poor, he teaches to support his parents and often does not have enough for himself to live on. Chi'an told me, "Nazhai is my best friend. We share each other's joys and sorrows, help each other in need, share our worries together. What prevents me from being united in one body with Nazhai is that he and I are like clouds—we are being blown hither and thither."

Visibly moved by my account, Danyuan added his praise for Nazhai's chivalry.

Mengzhan then asked about Ningxi. I told him:

Ningxi is naturally brilliant. He writes spontaneously in a vigorous and expansive manner. As a person he is warm-hearted, open and generous. When he encounters injustice, he acts to correct it. He always tries to help others solve their problems, but he never bothers others with his own troubles. Once he was without provisions but subsisted on weeds and cracked wheat porridge and went about walking in the snow with his head held high. He wrote a poem about that incident:

> Tracks of men and birds have vanished from view;
> Folded hills and sweeping woods lurk in the haze.
> With an old cloth tunic to resist the cold,
> I wear my coir cloak to walk in the Jiangnan snow.

Ningxi was once sent 20 *hu*[25] of rice by a military officer who wanted an essay for his mother's birthday. Ningxi wrote several thousand words for him in a flourish, astonishing everyone who was present.

Another time at a party, shrimps were served, and Ningxi was asked to write a poem about them. He first drank a cupful of wine and then wrote:

> Your beard's long, your eyes protrude, your mouth's a spear.
> Usually found at parties, you bow to be courteous.
> The straight path is no more, waists are easily bent.[26]
> It's a pity your horn head resembles that of a dragon.

Ningxi's brilliance sometimes caused people to think he is mad.

It was the day after we arrived at Chi'an's that Nazhai came, and

Ningxi came the day after. That was when I let Ningxi read Shuangqing's poetry from my *Sanji*. That evening, after midnight, he brought his lampstand to my room and pulling open my bed curtains, shouted, "Is there such a lady? She must be the embodiment of Heaven and Earth! Talented and beautiful, she stands up to poverty and sickness; on top of that she tolerates a terrible husband and a cruel mother-in-law roaring at her and pressuring her everyday. You'd expect her to die, yet she lingers on; you'd expect her to become resentful, yet she doesn't. On the contrary, she exhausts herself to work and carry out her filial duties as a wife and a daughter-in-law. This puts her above other ill-fated women with their talents and beauty, their poverty and sickness—none of them could compare with her. Her husband and mother-in-law should be thankful for their blessings!" He made an offering of some chrysanthemums to Shuangqing's painting, then played his flute in front of it. When he was through, he wept. He used the chrysanthemums to wipe his tears and laughingly said, "In the whole world nothing else is worthy of my tears!"

Ningxi sported long hair and some whiskers on the chin of his square face. He was wearing short sleeves. Under the lamp he danced around, laughing heartily. Time and time again he lifted my bed curtains and squatted in front of my bed with arms akimbo. His eyes were as bright as the morning stars and he talked without stopping.

Jing Zhenxiang 荊振翔 of Danyang copied Shuangqing's lyric verses, writing the whole night until dawn. He was only twenty but was talented and sensitive. He was handsome and gentle without the ostentatious flippancy of some young people. As a matter of fact, his manner was something like yours, Mengzhan.

Mengzhan asked if I met any worthy new acquaintances. I told him:

On the way north, Danyuan and I reached the town of Jinniu (金牛鎮) and stayed at the Sanli Shrine (三里菴). One of the fellow passengers in the boat was a monk from Cangcheng 蒼乘. When he viewed Shuangqing's painting, he pressed his hands together and muttered,

"Amida Buddha!" Another passenger who stayed behind to be with us was He Dingfu 賀定敷 from Jiangshu of Danyang [Shuangqing's native village]. When he read her poetry, he started to stamp his feet in the boat, scaring everybody. He was thinking of coming back with us to pay Shuangqing a visit but regretted that he could not take time off from his tutoring job. All of a sudden he stamped his feet again and said, "Oh, if I could only see Shuangqing, I would never have regrets again!" That night we stayed at Sanli Shrine. Dawn had yet to break when Dingfu came to me. With his face in a sweat, he was so irritated that he threw down his cap. He borrowed a brush from one of the monks to copy Shuangqing's poetry. He said he did not sleep the whole night, listening to the rain and kicking his feet in bed.

Zhang Laiyu 張萊娛 of Lücheng 呂城, the younger brother of a 1732 *xiaolian* 孝廉,[27] Zhang Xingjian 張星澗, was knowledgeable in the art of physiognomy. He also had a good voice. We arrived at Ningxi's on the ninth of the month and he arrived the next day. He asked Ningxi to accompany his singing with the flute. He viewed the painting of Shuangqing and said, "Her face is like the moon; her shadow is somewhat slight; her skin is like snow, and her color shows some depression. She is like the plum blossom goddess with bones of the lotus. She has cultivated talent and character. She is a goddess exiled on earth."

Ningxi's uncle, Du'an 度菴, had been sick in bed for ten years. But he painted landscapes in his curtained bed and asked poets to write inscriptions on his paintings. When he viewed the painting of Shuangqing, he warned Ningxi: "This person is from Heaven. You mustn't treat her painting with disrespect. You should burn incense before it." Du'an has compassion and nobility in his character, very much like Zhenting in my estimation.

He Shuangqing's Home Life

[1733] On the twentieth day of the tenth month I came back from Menghe. Shuangqing's malaria has persisted. The doctor said,

"There are eight stages in malaria, all caused by the patient's diet and temperature. During a fever, the heat from the cooking fire will produce sweat in the patient and then dry it up. The worst thing is to be chilled by wind and to eat when angry. When the patient's depression is not released, yet she forces herself to eat, this will only nourish the root of her malaria, a root which has been there earlier causing phlegm in the esophagus. The way to cure it is to release her depression, pacify her and remove her anxieties."

Shuangqing, though frail physically, maintains a good temper. She is very patient. Even when depressed, she shows herself to be calm and cheerful. When a sympathetic woman visitor in Shuangqing's room scolded and cursed Shuangqing's family about the way they treated her at home, Shuangqing pleaded with the woman to stop. The woman finally said, "Are you a dead toad? How can you be so cowardly?"

One day Shuangqing happened to pause for breath while she was pounding rice. Her husband immediately suspected her of loafing. He shoved her with force and, as she fell on the mortar, the pestle hit her waist. She endured the pain, got up and resumed pounding. Her husband glared at her angrily. She smiled to apologize, saying, "The grain should be ready for threshing now."

For lunch she made rice porridge and was half-way through when she had a flare-up of her malaria. The fire was too strong and so the porridge boiled over. She quickly added some water to the porridge. But her mother-in-law was already upon her, scolding and pulling her by her ear. She yanked at Shuangqing with such force that she tore off Shuangqing's earring, splitting her ear lobe. Shuangqing put a hand over her wounded ear and wept. With the ladle raised, the old woman threatened her, "How dare you cry!" Shuangqing had to wipe the pot and finish the cooking.

Her husband thought she had overstepped herself and so forbade her to eat lunch that day. Shuangqing continued pounding rice. A neighbor woman asked her, "Aren't you hungry?" She said, "No." The neighbor said, "You feel full because of the rage in you." Shuangqing scooped out the flour from the mortar, then touching the ground with her head [reverently] answered, "May Heaven let me bear all the suffering for all the ill-fated young women in the world so that none of them should ever have a fate like mine!"

Therefore, she asked the servant boy Ling to copy my *Sanji* for her so that when she dies, it will be buried with her. She wrote "Nine Poems Harmonizing Bailuo" with rouge on a handkerchief. When Mengzhan asked to see the poems, she declined saying, "You will not understand this, but if I were destined to be another ill-fated beauty in my next life, I would want to be another Shuangqing!" I was given the chance to copy her poems, after which I hastened to return her handkerchief. On it I detected some water spots, which no doubt were tear stains.

Nine Poems Harmonizing Bailuo (和白羅九首)

I.

Since I can't fulfill my vow
Of retiring to a nunnery,
My frozen heart is impassive
Like a still pool.
Don't blame the hungry swallow
For being late at building his nest;
When the cocoon silk is thin,
Who pities the sick silkworm?

未許焚修閉小菴，冰心無皺似澄潭。
泥遲枉怪饑時燕，繭薄誰憐病後蠶。

II.

This year's ample rain
Cuts off the autumn clouds.

As usual I pawn my skirt
To make up for the next rent.
Since I can preserve the padded jacket
To keep my husband warm,
My heart is like honey,
I don't reject him.

今年膏雨斷秋雲，爲補新租又典裙。
留得護郎輕絮煖，妾心如蜜敢嫌君。

III.

Stitching closely to make a pair of hemp boots
Calls for many layers of thread.
To pick kindling tomorrow
I'll go up the west peak.
The sudden chill in the night
Is accompanied by a fierce wind—
Don't blow at my husband,
Concentrate on me.

細納麻鞵線幾重，采樵明日上西峯。
乍寒一夜風偏急，莫向郎吹盡向儂。

IV.

Smoky and damp, the cold kitchen
Is on the lower level.
Using *wutong* wood for fuel
Calls for an apology to the phoenix.[28]
I pick weeds for greens,
In the cold I wash them;
The chrysanthemum may suffer,
What can you do about the frost?

冷廚烟濕障低房，爨盡梧桐謝鳳凰。
野菜自挑寒自洗，菊花雖痛奈何霜。

V.

My life is fragile
Like a cicada's wing.
I used to be as beautiful
As the neighbor's daughter—
When Mother sees me,
Will she recognize her child
Now that bitter yellow has robbed
My face of its cheerful pink?

命如蟬翼愧輕綃，舊與鄰娥一樣嬌。
阿母見兒還認否？苦黃生面喜紅消。

VI.

Deluged by spring's tempering
Is my little heart;
In illness dreams are infrequent—
They fade easily.
Having pawned my mirror,
Gold hairpins to buy medicine,
I must whittle some willow branches
To pin up my hair by the reflection of the water.

浸透春酸一點心，病中疏夢易銷沉。
鏡釵已賣酬方藥，自削楊枝照水簪。

VII.

The shadow of Siping Mountain is cast
Far out like a plateau.
My husband has been hauling wood
Up and down in the cold.
When he returns, I shall plead
With him to sleep late;
Even when the sun is up,
I will not let anyone disturb him.

四屏山影遠如臺，郎負寒薪下幾回。
歸後勸郎晨晏起，日高私禁外人催。

VIII.

The family chickens are happily paired:
They go about wing to wing,
Shoulder to shoulder, comb to comb.
Yet when the lamp dims, its wick turns to a bud,
Its flame takes on a greenish hue,
I choose to lean on the stove
Rather than on the railing
[Where the chickens can be seen].

家雞雙宿笑棲鸞，比翼齊肩並紫冠。
燈暗結花光變綠，竈稜堪倚勝闌干。

IX.

I live next to a painted house
Behind a humble door.
When the scent of the tuberose wafts over,
I'm sad behind the screen.
I have depleted my feelings
For the autumn's glow;
Fading grass, setting sun
Make me dream of going far away.

妾住衡門傍綵樓，夜香吹下隔簾愁。
袖開落盡秋紅句，衰草殘陽夢遠遊。

He Shuangqing's Conversation with a Neighbor and Her Letter to Her Uncle

A neighbor woman asked Shuangqing, "Your fate is so wretched, why do you want to live?" Shuangqing replied, "This is some old debt from a former life. If I don't pay it in this life, it will be visited upon me in my next life. Look at the men in the village, many are fools and are insensitive in their human relationships. They are worse off than my husband. My mother-in-law, though exacting, still acts decently toward me when I carry out my duties and serve her with care. I won't dare look forward to anything beyond that. People say I am ill-fated, but that's because they think I have talent and beauty. After all, there are many untalented and ordinary looking girls around, they too would like to have good husbands. I am not alone in this wish. Beauty and talent are given to me by Heaven to destroy me. If I should commit suicide to carry out the will of Heaven, I'd be very foolish indeed."

The neighbor said, "Many scholars' wives have affairs outside. Why are you so cautious?" Shuangqing said, "The poor eat unhusked grain everyday, yet they feel ashamed to steal meat. In other words, though meat is superior to unhusked grain, still it is not worth stealing. Now if you steal something of similar worth, you commit a crime. You soil your own body and insult both families; one moment's foolishness brings a hundred years of shame. You fall in one little thing and everything else goes with it. I may be ignorant, but I can't make myself do that."

The woman then said, "Why do you let your poetry be circulated then?" With tears in her eyes, Shuangqing said, "This is what they describe as 'The lotus inherits its nature and its silk is difficult to sever.' With all the emotions constantly welling up in me, my poetry simply comes by itself. I want the ill-fated beauties in the world to use me as an example, not to blame themselves but to value poetry and education and practice propriety in order to keep themselves chaste for the sake of their parents and the future generations. If I can do this, then I will not have lived in vain."

On the twenty-sixth day of the tenth month she cut a three inch rush leaf and wrote a letter on it to her uncle in these words:

Everybody says it is my fate to be cast into such miserable circumstances. Actually my life is not that miserable. Countless young women from good, rich families perish in their inner chambers. The evening brings them no joy, and when facing spring they find it hard to express their sorrow. The peach blossoms are beautiful, but die early; the bamboo is only a green plant, but it can endure poverty. This is worth our observation. These young women often have to follow superstitious traditions, seldom get any praise, they are like bright pearls cast into black waters. When a resentful bird makes its last sound and repairs its faded feathers, it may still be appreciated by the bard. Yet here are fragrant orchids that are regarded as worthless things. When I wrote the poems on the chrysanthemum and the lonely wild goose, people said I was resentful. I am without virtue, naturally I cannot be without resentment, and yet I know I do not resent my husband. Xiao Qing[29] of the Ming dynasty cared only to be united with her lover. As for me, I only want to become a man in my next life. I shall be content to spend the rest of my life in *Chan* meditation and chanting Buddhist sutras.

Shuangqing always used pollen on leaves, and not ink on paper, to write her poetry. The reason might be that leaves crumble easily and pollen without glue drops off; she did not want to have her handwriting handed down.

More on He Shuangqing's Life and Poetry

The painting of Shuangqing washing clothes, which I took to Menghe, circulated among the scholars there. They sang their praises about her. Chi'an wrote a lyric to the tune of *Man jiang hong* 滿江紅 , Chao Nazhai did a seven-character regulated verse, and Ningxi did a seven-character ancient poem for her. Shuangqing responded to this with her "After Ningxi's Rhyme" (步寧溪韻), which reads:

I.

Moonlight trickles its brilliance
Onto the slope of Xiaoshan,
Splinters the sunset's glow
Into choked ice, it seems.
The pink mist ascending,
Becomes elegant clouds;
It turns the whole sky
Into lotus hues.

月魂滴豔綃山側，細切霞膏嘸冰臆。
紅粉蒸爲窈窕雲，青天盡變芙蓉色。

II.

My abode is in Huayang's[30]
Eighth heaven,
On the west a brook,
On the south a field.
I finger the fine silk
Tender as rain—
I long to use it
In match-making[31] for the true lovers.

家住華陽第八天，舍西流水舍南田。
手撚香絲嫩如雨，欲繫鴛鴦問可憐。

III.

My face is haggard,
My husband's creased.
The dust in the little court is chalky,
Difficult to sweep away.
The peony impoverished
Yields no bloom;
Instead, it relinquishes
Its nutrients to the herbs.

妾容憔悴郎顏老，小庭土白塵難掃。
牡丹貧賤不成花，卻將富貴輸芳草。

IV.

I recall how in the mulberry shade
I learned to plant melons,
Quenched my husband's thirst
By offering him tea.
In the cool night while sick,
I'd sit at the open window,
Let in the moonlight by blowing out the lamp
To weave hemp in the dark.

曾記桑陰學種瓜，與郎消渴餉郎茶。
夜涼帶病開窗坐，放月吹燈暗績麻。

V.

The scholars came to appreciate talent
But received little response from me;
Now I'm peacefully
Settled in a farm family.
After the rain
The oriole's sudden cry
Summons my spring sorrow
Into the green, green arbor.

書生漫負憐才癖，妾在田家靜安帖。
雨後黃鸝乍一聲，春愁喚上青青葉。

VI.

Impending snow, cloudy or sunny,
Becomes the evening's riddle;
In front of my bed
There's no space for pacing.
Even if I could become

A lonely phoenix,
I'd not fly
To the Jade Pavilion of Qin.[32]

雪意陰晴向晚猜，牀前無地可徘徊。
縱教化作孤飛鳳，不到秦家弄玉臺。

VII.

The constellation is askew,
Only remnants remain.
Mending a winter jacket
Entails much sewing.
Dreamily the white mist
Embraces the plum blossoms;
Thick frost bathes
My face in the night air.

斜羅仄布零星片，自綻寒衣費針線。
白烟遮夢抱梅花，繁霜夜洗佳人面。

Mengzhan and Renzhi went to collect rent in the western mountains. The harvest was poor, so most of the farm tenants were starving. Mengzhan and Renzhi took only fifty percent of the rent grain from them and thirty percent from the widows, widowers and the sick. There was a woman recently widowed who had no quilted clothes. When they arrived, she clutched her child to her bosom and wept at the stove. She took the rent grain out from under her bed. They took only half of the discounted amount which was just enough for the government taxes, leaving the rest for her and the child.

In the evening they returned to Xiaoshan and dropped in at Shuangqing's. She washed some cups and warmed some white wine for them. Mengzhan told her, "We just returned from the mountains with a poem. If you could harmonize it, I'll present you with some grain we have in the boat." Shuangqing immediately came up with a regulated verse, "Harmonizing Mengzhan" (和夢覘):

> The wind sweeps fine rain,
> Wetting the rustic gate.
> There's little to do
> In the ten *mu*[33] of paddy field.
> The weather's been dry;
> The cotton's yet to bloom;
> The shuttles are cold;
> I lean on the empty loom.
> 風吹細雨濕柴扉，十畝溪田事業微。
> 歲旱木棉花未發，杼寒梭冷倚空機。

When they offered her the grain, she would not accept it, saying, "To exchange a poem for grain, that's shameful."

There is a laborer, Qian Qinglang 錢磬郎 , who works with Shuangqing's husband. He saw his own image in the pond and thought himself handsome. With his wages he bought a purple tunic, a black felt hat, and black slippers. He washed his face, brushed his teeth, shaved his head, rubbed himself with oil and went about singing love ditties. He tried to look gentle while he gave his rendition. Making some excuse, he borrowed something from Shuangqing and held it carefully in his hand. Shuangqing told him to stop his foolishness. This made him sheepish, so he immediately took off his tunic and slippers and sold them. From then on, whenever he came within sight of Shuangqing, he dared not look at her.

Shuangqing pleaded with her husband to give up gambling. This made him so angry that he locked her in the woodshed. She leaned on the wood and wept. Watching a lamp, she wrote "The Dying Lamp Wick" (殘燈) to the tune of *Fenghuang tai shang yi chuixiao* 鳳凰臺上憶吹簫 :

Already dim but left unblown,
You want to brighten but who'll pull you up?
You face me like a firefly without a flame.
Listen to the cold rain on the tamped-earth steps—
It'll drip through the third watch.
Alone, placid, yet disquiet,
You're undecided,
Because you are too emotional.
Your oil is exhausted,
But your heart is still warm.
Stay awhile to keep me company.

You're now a spark,
You're getting smaller, languishing.
I hope while you linger,
You will flare.
It's better than being the fisherman's lamp,
Wavering in the wind on the open sea,
Toiling in the trail of autumn moths.
I'm already sick,
Will not improve.
After gazing at you for a while,
I may doze off
To sleep away my empty fears.

已暗忘吹，欲明誰剔？向儂無燄如螢。聽土階寒雨，滴破三更。獨自懨懨耿耿，難斷處，也忒多情。香膏盡，芳心未冷，且伴雙卿。　　星星，漸微不動。還望你淹煎，有個花生。勝野塘風亂，搖曳漁燈，辛苦秋蛾散後。人已病，病減何曾？相看久，朦朧成睡，睡去空驚。

On the fifth day of the eleventh month, I was in Mengzhan's studio, browsing through some Tang poetry. It had been raining for nearly ten days and the steps were covered with fallen leaves. I went outside to take a look. The sky was covered with cumulus clouds, blending heaven and earth into one color.

Mengzhan told me that Shuangqing's husband went to the mountain to cut wet wood for fuel. He said that Shuangqing is subsisting on leeks and taro. She is also secretly exchanging taro for rice to make porridge for her mother-in-law. She has been trying to cure herself by experimenting with different prescriptions. The result is that she suffers from complications. Mengzhan thought she must be very depressed and could be praying for an end to her life. Therefore, he wrote a letter to comfort her. It read:

> Anshu was only one year old when he lost his father, and eleven when he lost his mother. He stayed with relatives and often lacked food and clothing. When he was sixteen he returned to his old home to live by himself. He bought a cat and a dog for companionship, feeding them in the morning and the night. When he went out, he took the dog along but locked the cat at home. For three years he had chronic malaria. During its last flare-up he ate some solid food and kept some soup warm on the fire in front of his bed. He shut the door and tried to sleep off the malaria. When he got thirsty, he drank the soup. The cat sat by his pillow and made noise now and then. The dog lay in front of his bed, not moving. His malaria left him after that night. The next day he was hungry but found he was too weak to get up and cook for himself. The cat starved to death and he wrote a poem for her:
>
> When I come home, only you welcome me;
> When I go out, you suffer hunger.
> Now the dog is hurt and I can't take care of myself;
> You look at me and make a few feeble sounds.
>
> Anshu could write poetry at the age of nine. He traveled around the Lake Ge (滆湖) area and on some days he would not eat at all. Wherever he went he wrote poetry. Once he spent the night in an ancient temple, where he wrote a poem on the wall:
>
> The autumn's gloom and the evening's darkness
> Make the road ahead difficult to see.
> Behind the smartweed the shadowy boat is hidden;

The pine is tall and the deserted temple, empty.
Emotions of the traveler rise with the festival at hand;
The wayfarer's progress is the same every year.
The ancient way no one talks of anymore,
One hears only the faint rustling of the grain.

Anshu wrote this poem for a friend:

Fate pities the young woman;
Poverty makes one think of children.
Love brings difficult days;
Emotions rise when people part from one another.

During a bout with malaria, he stayed in an abandoned kiln. He took a piece of lime and wrote this poem on the kiln wall entitled "Written on the Wall":

Painful recollections,
Is there anyone to share them with me?
Often my lonely heart
Is as dreary as autumn,
It is not that I am not ambitious,
It is just that encumbering feelings
Bring great sadness
At all times.

The kiln is now sealed, but the poem on the deserted temple wall still remains.

At thirty Anshu was again very sick. The following year he met me. Since that time he has not been sick as often. Sometimes he regrets that he did not meet me earlier, for as soon as he did meet me, his malaria disappeared completely. Anshu is such a brilliant scholar, still Heaven has given him so much hardship. You are a most talented beauty; perhaps Heaven is doing the same to you.

For this reason Shuangqing wrote "Ode to Malaria" (咏瘧) to the tune of *Boxing* 薄倖 . She said, "Anshu is sickly, Yuhan is poor. To have both sickness and poverty, that's me. On top of all this, I am a woman. How sad!" She added, "It'd indeed be a blessing for me to turn into a colorful cloud and float away!" Her poem reads:

Abiding with me is my lonely shadow;
I'm confused as in a dream—
Who'll wake me?
I endure much scolding from the butterfly,
Ire from the bee;
No wonder that even with medicine
I don't improve.
During the harvest season
Is there a moment for rest?
Mournfully I rekindle the brazier
To brew my medicine.

On the whole I've unfolded my sorrows,
Exhausted my tears.
No one knows the killing oppression I suffer—
Getting through the evening,
Facing the midday,
The day drags and night is forever.
Just after much turning
When I'm about to fall asleep,
It's time to rise again.

The sad honking of the wild geese
Breaks the sunset's afterglow,
Chilling it.
The evening hill is like a mirror;
The small rustic gate
In the shrouding mist confines me.
I believe my shortness of breath will soon cease.
How I wish spring will return early;
My only fear—the east wind may not agree.

依依孤影，渾似夢，憑誰喚醒？受多少蝶嗔蜂怒，有藥難醫花證。最忙時，那得工夫？淒涼自整紅爐等。　　總訴盡濃愁，滴乾清淚。寃煞蛾眉不省，去過酉，來先午，便放卻更深宵永。正千迴萬轉，欲眠仍起。　　斷鴻叫破殘陽冷，晚山如鏡。小柴扉，烟鎖佳人，翠袖懨懨病。春歸望早，只恐東風未肯。

Scholar Zhu Xiye

Zhu Xiye 朱西野 was a Cantonese; his grandfather was an official in Jintan and so Xiye remained here. He could not take the Jintan district examination which was reserved for their native sons, but with the recommendation of Yu Erjie 于爾喈,[34] he was allowed to take the prefectural one, which he passed with a first rank. He was harrassed by many who were jealous of him. He soon fell sick but could not afford a doctor. Hu Dahu 胡達湖 doctored him. Xiye tried to compensate Hu for the service by pawning some of his possessions, but Hu would not accept any money. At that time I was studying with Master Yu at his Shuanggui Studio (雙桂堂). Every evening Dahu, Shushan 墅山, and I went out of the city to see Xiye. We would leave only at the last bell.

When Xiye got a little better, he was able to leave his sickbed, and wearing only a pair of clogs on his feet, saw me off in the snow when I went back to Guazhu. He wrote a poem for me with the lines: "Unconventional writing is shamefully passed over; / Friendship despite poverty brings tears of gold." He stood at the river bank to watch my boat move far away before turning back. The following year in the sixth month he died at the young age of thirty. Shushan sent me the elegy he wrote for Xiye, and I went to offer a sacrifice at his grave.

Well-to-do at the beginning, Xiye was tempted by his merchant friends with women, wine and gambling. When he exhausted his money, he made up his mind to concentrate on his studies. He wrote poetry and prose and became a friend of Shushan, while those former friends in the city all abandoned him. Often depressed, he wrote a long autobiographical poem entitled "The Willow Catkins" to voice his regrets and remorse. He and I had known each other for only three years when he died.

The servant boy Ling brought the first fifteen stanzas of Xiye's "The Willow Catkins" to show Shuangqing. She was pounding rice. She held the pestle to her bosom and glancing at the title, smiled and exclaimed, "A poem entitled 'The Willow Catkins,' a subject not easy to versify." In the process of reading she was choked with emotion a few times. When she finished, she muttered to herself. "Just imagine! In this world of dust there was such a heart-broken person! The poem's compassion and feeling of futility in speaking out resemble the *Li sao* 離騷;[35] its grasp on perspective is like the *Nanhua*;[36] its liberation is like the *Lengyan jing* 楞嚴經.[37] 'The Willow Catkins' has finally found a bosom friend."

When Ling showed her the remaining fifteen stanzas of Xiye's "The Willow Catkins," Shuangqing had resumed pounding rice. She turned her head to ask what poetry it was, and Ling told her it was also on the willow catkins. She then asked, "Who did this?" Ling said, "Also Xiye." She sat on the mortar to read it. After reading it, she shuddered and changed color. She merely said, "But this is me!"

[Note: Zhu Xiye's "The Willow Catkins" is too long for translation. In essence, it says that the remorse Zhu felt over the futility of his life in the material world finally liberated him to seek his own selfhood. He Shuangqing's empathy with the spirit of Zhu's poem shows that she was sympathetic toward all fellow human beings, not only other women in similar predicament as herself.]

Scholar Friends Visiting Xiaoshan

The winter solstice fell on the seventeenth day of the eleventh month. Ningxi and Nazhai came to Jintan to visit Wang Danyuan, and all three of them came to Xiaoshan the following day. When Ningxi saw Master Xiuyuan and his sons, Mengzhan and Renzhi, he saluted them saying, "You gentlemen are good-hearted, you protect what Heaven loves. You are benevolent." Xiuyuan did not understand what he meant. Ningxi explained: "Heaven does not place Shuangqing anywhere other than under your roof in order to protect her. If she didn't live here, wouldn't she be thrown to the wolves?" He then told me, "You are the jade ladder to the ironclad mountain. Shuangqing may be beautiful and talented; still, her work could have benefited from your editing. I would like to see one of the leaves on which she writes her poetry to allay my suspicion." Instead, I showed him the ten or more poems written for Shuangqing by Qian Lingxiao 錢凌宵 and Zheng Chi'an, as testimonies from these scholars. Lingxiao, also named Laicheng 來成 and Daji 大濟, was a prodigy. He lives the Dao and teaches with understanding; Chi'an treats him like a master. Both Danyuan and Lingxiao have written inscriptions on the painting of Shuangqing washing clothes.

Ningxi wrote a poem whose rhyme Shuangqing used for her poem, "After Ningxi's Rhyme." Ningxi thought she did a better job with it than he and so tried to write another poem using the same rhyme but did not succeed. Now he wanted to test Shuangqing. He asked us for suggestions of subject matter. We decided on these subjects: "The Plantain" as suggested by Ningxi, "The Heavenly Bamboo" as suggested by Nazhai, and "Snow Clearing over the Western Mountains" as suggested by Danyuan.

In the evening they sent these titles to Shuangqing. Before dawn her poems arrived. They were done in seven-character ancient rhymes. She had written them on one square inch of rush leaf with very thin ink, rendering them almost indistinct. Her poems read:

The Plantain (芣苢)

The more the scattered clouds try to right themselves,
The more they are blown askew;
Through their clefts they let in the last rays
To express my feelings.
Bianhe[38] shed tears
Over Jingshan to mourn
Flowers with their hidden beauty
Not perceived by the common man.
零雲欲正吹還側，隙送殘暉印孤臆。
卞和雙淚落荊山，百花暗帶消魂色。

The Heavenly Bamboo (天竹子)

Wet firewood smothers easily;
Winter vegetables are old.
Matted leaves, finally dry,
Are swept to the bamboo fence;
Under the stove are stored
Strands and strands of grass
In tight bundles
Hand-bound for fuel.
濕薪易滅寒蔬老，敗葉初乾向籬掃。
竈下絲絲縷縷存，盡是綢繆手中草。

Snow Clearing over the Western Mountains (西山雪霽)

The clouds in shavings
Have now vanished.
The lady adds another thread
To her embroidery.
Plantain is difficult to find,
Bamboo shoots are scarce;
Snow lifts, happily unveiling

The face of the western mountains.
香魂是片今非片，刺繡佳人又添線。
芣苢難尋竹實稀，雪晴幸見西山面。

Ningxi wanted to see Shuangqing. He asked Mengzhan to point her out to him, but the latter refused. So he walked up and down, saw some young beauties but decided that none of them was Shuangqing. Then he saw a young woman in old clothes drawing water. He was so astonished by her appearance that he knew immediately that that was Shuangqing. It had just been raining and he was standing in the mud with his shoes immersed, yet he was unaware of it.

He Shuangqing and Scholar Yuhan

Yuhan is poverty stricken. Even in winter he wears only a single layer of clothing. He walks briskly in the wind and shows no sign of being cold. He has hocked the quilted tunic given him by Mengzhan to buy medicine. He loves to sit up at night, even in winter. He does a good job of copying books and often has frozen fingers from doing so when it is cold. When he sits in a room, he can ignore the presence of others.

Shuangqing does not wear enough either. She lets her husband use her quilted jacket. Her husband's suit is her own work, made of cotton, woven by her and sewn beautifully. During the winter lull, he holds onto his crockery brazier, sips white wine and drunkenly exposes his back to the sun by the bamboo fence. When he is hungry or thirsty, he simply calls for Shuangqing to serve him. If it should get cold, she rekindles his brazier and warms him some wine. She also serves her mother-in-law with great respect.

One day at four in the afternoon Yuhan was out viewing the

western mountains. Shuangqing saw him from within her door. She told Ling, "Mr. Duan looks as if his clothing doesn't have any quilting in it. I have some hemp I could use to pad it for him. Will you bring me his clothing?" Ling told her that was not possible, as Yuhan owns but one set. Shuangqing therefore quoted the poem written to the tune of *Taichang yin* 太常引 which I wrote in 1728 when I took my young cousin, Zhuoren 卓人, to visit Anshu but did not find him at home. That poem reads:

> The lady is worried that the journey is long and difficult for me,
> That the wind and snow require heavier clothing.
> The sun is setting on Ji mountain,
> I first go to look at the plum blossoms leaning on the rail.
> Half a volume of my tear stained poetry
> I have brought to show Master Zhao.
> How can I leave with nothing accomplished?
> Dreary is the first night of being alone.

I remember when I set off to visit Anshu that time, my wife stopped me saying, "The days are getting short and the trip is long. The cold mist is like rain, the northern wind is fierce, and your old quilt has no warmth. I wish you wouldn't go." Finally she opened up my quilt and added some new cotton before letting me go. My tunic was remade with all the stitching replaced. The new cotton kept me warm.

Yuhan sent Shuangqing a poem written to the tune of *Huan xi sha* 浣溪沙. She responded with a lyric poem. He was so happy he could not sleep. Then he wrote her another lyric poem and she responded with my *Taichang yin* poem. He was beside himself with happiness. Another poem of hers that he received was written to the tune of *Yijian mei* 一剪梅. It reads:

> Chills, fevers come like tides—
> My condition is not stable.
> Speechless after a bout,

Alone I sweep the front court.
Tangerine flowers have faded,
Sky a mournful blue.
I push away my sorrows,
I'm alone.

When the evening is chilly,
Even the wild cock becomes lazy about crowing.
Will it snow, will it frost?
I fear rain, I hope for sunshine.
When things are quiet,
That's when I'm busy.
One instant, I'm happy;
Another, I'm scolded.

寒熱如潮勢未平。病起無言，自掃前庭。瓊花魂斷碧天愁，推下淒涼，一箇雙卿。　　夜冷荒雞嬾不鳴。擬雪猜霜，怕雨貪晴。最閒時候妾偏忙，纔喜雙卿，又怒雙卿。

That was the beginning of the twelfth month. The evening before that Shuangqing was sweeping willow leaves at her door. She was wearing a single layer of hemp clothing and had her hair in an old kerchief. She was suffering from malaria but kept to her relaxed and genial appearance. Her eyes glistened and her beauty shone. Yuhan walked back and forth to look at her. That night he became delirious. When he received this poem, he became more so. He then wrote a poem with the lines: "My spring dream was preposterous; / Nightingales and swallows, / They flitted about busily."

On account of this, Shuangqing wrote him a letter with pollen on *Reineckia carnea* leaves (吉祥葉):

Yesterday a neighbor woman heard that I wanted to sew some hemp into your clothes and she made fun of me. I told her, "Yuhan is over fifty, I'm but twenty-one. I have fallen into a dry well and don't even see the sun and the moon. There are also scorpions around. Yuhan sympathizes with me, he prostrates himself over the well and has been saying Amida Buddha for me day and night. He weeps and grieves for me even more than my own parents. I thank him in the well by touching my forehead to the ground; I could die without regrets.

"People in general are unfeeling, but Shi Zhenlin's friends are all warm-hearted. They are kind and filial, they are noble-minded and lean toward *Chan* Buddhism. If the world were in trouble, they would take it as their business, they would let down their hair and never dream of closing their doors to those in trouble. Yes, Yuhan has human heartedness and he does not transgress propriety. However, he does not let the decorum of separating males from females constrain him, for he is replete with the good heart of a parent. As for me, I am not an ordinary country woman, hiding from good people and relatives to keep company with only the lowly. I am open, sincere, I am not secretive in my actions. I don't admire lovers who dig holes in walls to meet one another.

"Also in this era of peace within the country there is no unmarried male or female, everyone has his or her own mate. I carry out my wifely duties in serving my farmer husband; I help to plant rice and never leave his side. Every evening I give thanks to the emperor, wishing him ten thousand years; I burn incense to thank Heaven. I have never ceased in these observations.

"I'm given the gift of being a poet and it's true that occasionally I communicate with the gentlemen. Although my work is poor, nevertheless, I hope people who collect poetry will not think of me as being forward. The gentlemen are compassionate, I know that well. If they were to go beyond that, it would be too intimate; if they were effusive, it would be beyond good manners. I treasure myself like a piece of jade and they do not waste their ink. They treasure it like gold."

After reading this letter, Yuhan said, "This does it. Now I am reduced to a child!" His delirium became violent, he shouted and scolded. When he woke up, he said, "I'm poor and old. Only because of Shuangqing am I able to forget both. If I withhold my compassion from her, how should I spend it? There hasn't been a mad, compassionate person in the world for a long time. Let it be me!"

He Shuangqing and Han Xi

[1733] On the eighth day of the twelfth month, I left Xiaoshan to go home to pack for a northern trip. I comforted Shuangqing and told her to take care of herself by not letting her toil and worries worsen her health. I have resolved to devote my northern trip to spreading her name.

Shuangqing's friend, Han Xi 韓西, came home to visit her parents after her marriage. Whenever she found Shuangqing pounding rice or hauling water, she would help her. When Shuangqing was sick with malaria, Han Xi would sit by her bed and weep. Intelligent though illiterate, she loved Shuangqing's calligraphy. She begged Shuangqing to write the *Xin jing* for her and teach her to recite it. When Han Xi was preparing to return to her husband's home, her parents gave her a dinner and invited Shuangqing, but the latter could not attend on account of her malaria. Han Xi refused to eat that day. She kept half of her food for Shuangqing.

Shuangqing was touched by this and so wrote a poem to the tune of *Mo yuer* 摸魚兒 for Han Xi:

> Glad the rain has stopped,
> Sunset aglow in the west;
> Cold mountains beyond the mist in gradations of blue and green.
> Where it's dry on the moss I can tread,
> Leaving traces on the mud still soft and purple.
> Too much noise here;
> I'd better go lean on the rustic gate.

I haven't fulfilled my deep wish—
Our love is of one thread,
I'll twist it into a thread under the new moon,
Use it to string all my sorrows and regrets
In the way my pearly tears do fall.

After twilight
I'm still feverish—who'll pity my panting?
Through the small window the wind shoots like arrows.
Blooming spring, elegant autumn, both beautiful, but without emotion.
Rare is the flower like myself.
Our meeting will be distant;
I've heard that the broken heart
Has already accepted the farewell feast.
The low sun hurts my eyes,
I mustn't gaze at the horizon anymore—
After all, there are only
A few cold clouds expanding on the horizon.

喜初晴，晚霞西現，寒山烟外青淺。苔紋乾處容香履，尖印紫泥猶軟。人語亂，忙去倚柴扉。空負深深願。相思一線，向新月搓圓，穿愁貫恨，珠淚總成串。　　黃昏後，殘熱誰憐細喘？小窗風射如箭。春紅秋白無情豔，一朵似儂難選。重見遠，聽說道，傷心已受殷勤餞。斜陽刺眼，休更望天涯，天涯只是，幾片冷雲展。

Shuangqing also wrote a poem on a bamboo leaf to the tune of *Fenghuang tai shang yi chuixiao* 鳳凰臺上憶吹簫 with thin ink in small writing:

Tiny, tiny snippets of clouds,
Silky, silky strands of sunset's afterglow.
They are, they are not; they glow, they will not cease.
Just when they affect my spirit, my spirit gives way.
How they glitter and sway!

Look, look! Hill after hill, water after water!
When a person dies,
His spirit hovers, hovers among the rushes far, far away.
From now on
My life will be sour, sour, bitter, bitter—
Just like tonight.

Oh, blue yonder.
I've asked Heaven but received no reply.
Look at little, little Shuangqing,
Weak, weak, ennui.
Who do I see, who sees me?
Who feels tenderly for beautiful flowers?
Who looks forward happily, happily,
Secretly using pollen
To write, write, sketch, sketch?
Who would care life after life, generation after generation,
Dusk after dusk, dawn after dawn?

寸寸微雲，絲絲殘照，有無明滅難消。正斷魂魂斷，閃閃搖搖。望望山山水水，人去去，隱隱迢迢。從今後，酸酸楚楚，只似今宵。　青遙，問天不應。看小小雙卿，嬝嬝無聊。更見誰誰見？誰痛花嬌？誰望歡歡喜喜，偷素粉，寫寫描描？誰還管，生生世世，夜夜朝朝？

He Shuangqing's Letter to Shi Zhenlin

I had planned to return to Guazhu on Lake Tao on the tenth, but it began to rain so hard that I did not go. On the evening of the eleventh I discussed my *Sanji* with Yuhan. Emotionally I closed my manuscript and said, "There are so many things in this world that tax our emotions. People who like my writing may suspect its contents. Those who are bound by logic may find fault with what I have written. For this reason I feel disheartened. I wouldn't care if this manuscript were burned."

Yuhan agreed, "I could see that Shuangqing doesn't let convention bind her. I've never found a woman like her in history. Perhaps you should eliminate some of your entries about her in your book."

I said, "I've actually burned ten books of old manuscripts at Weiyang 維揚 already. I suppose I should also burn this *Xiqing sanji*. A person's span of life is very short; if he doesn't cultivate the salvation of his soul, that will be the end of that person. When you look at life this way, how insignificant are the speech and writing of a person."

When Shuangqing heard about this conversation, she wrote me a letter:

> When I was fifteen, I heard my uncle lecture on the *Shi jing* 詩經 (Book of Poetry). He objected to the fact that the sections of "Zhounan" 周南 and "Zhaonan" 召南 , done mostly by women, and the "Zhengfeng" 鄭風 and "Weifeng" 衛風 ,[39] which are love songs, were not censored by Confucius when the sage edited the collection. He also thought that Confucius' disciples should have objected to their inclusion. He wished he had been a disciple of Confucius so he could have corrected the Master on this. I told him he was only fit to be a disciple of Zaiyu 宰予 [the student of Confucius who napped in the afternoon and thus incurred the Master's disapproval], and he should learn to take afternoon naps.
>
> My uncle said that if he were a disciple of Confucius, he would have had the Master censor two stories in the records:[40] one, of the man who begged and got drunk at funeral sacrifices and then boasted of having been wined and dined by friends when he got home; the other, of the father who was hauled to court by his son for stealing a chicken. To him these stories were exaggerations, if not fabrications. I told him that he had a long way to go to become the moralist he envisioned himself to be.
>
> To me the Dao has no formal formula, the great learning does not lock one in. Teaching the village children *Doctrine of the Mean* (中庸),[41] a teacher may earnestly think he is the best exponent of

Confucianism and Neo-Confucianism. Actually his pupils may be all dozing while he lectures. I have secretly observed this and think it a great farce. I think the teacher is befuddled by his own deafness and blindness.

Now you are becoming cautious of everything. You talk loftily but you act otherwise. You dwell on unimportant things, allowing yourself to be like a windlass. I don't approve of it.

If you burn your manuscript, perhaps you should also refrain from speaking. The butterfly does not speak, yet it loves flowers; the maggot does not speak, yet it eats feces. Those who keep quiet to fool people into thinking they are wise, if they are fragrant, they are butterflies; if not, they are maggots.

Such things frustrate me and cause my malaria to worsen. As far as I'm concerned, I'm but a dream. What is worthy in the dream is not constant. When I wake up and think about it, I have no regrets. Whether you understand me or condemn me, please don't take this correspondence as the reason.

He Shuangqing and Anshu

On the eleventh day of the third month, I went into the city to visit a priest friend, Zhu Yuanming 朱元明, in the northern part of the city. Cao Jisan 曹及三 came and presented me with a copy of his poetry collection, which is imbued with simplicity and purity. He and I went to visit Wang Danyuan who lives in the southern part of town. We were leaning on some bamboo and talking when suddenly we heard someone reciting Danyuan's poetry in a clear voice. I said, "That's Anshu." We cut across the bamboo grove to have a look and found Anshu and Yu Quhu 于屈湖 engaged in conversation on top of the city wall overlooking the moat. Anshu called to me saying, "I've just come from Xiaoshan and I am planning to return to East Lake tomorrow." Then he added, "Mengzhan saw me off and was looking for you." On the thirteenth day Mengzhan invited me to visit Xiaoshan again. Anshu sighed and said, "Xiaoshan I'd love to see again, but I can't bear to see Shuangqing. Two days ago I requested a poem from her. She hesitated because she was afraid it would sadden me. I was inconsiderate in sending her a poem of my own, and even now I regret my action." Nevertheless, he accompanied Danyuan and me to Xiaoshan.

Anshu became more depressed, he had no interest in living. When he heard people reciting Shuangqing's poetry, he would say he wanted to die. He said that in the eighth month of the past year, he had returned to East Lake and sat among the rushes to cry his heart out. Still, he felt he had not expressed his feelings fully. He wanted to be able to sit in front of Shuangqing and cry for three days and three nights in order to rid himself of all his sadness about her. That day he received a letter from Shuangqing, beautifully worded. It told of her inner thoughts and contained the line: "A single word from the immortal is greater than an ever-luminescent pearl."

Anshu held onto the letter and started crying. Suddenly we lost sight of him, only to find him in the Niu Pavilion (牛亭). He was lying there with a stone for his pillow. We had to persuade him to come back with us. The next day he disappeared again. This happened three times. He would lift his eyes to heaven, sigh and say, "Scholar Zhao does not want to live anymore!" Danyuan laughed at him for being mad. Anshu told him, "I'm not biased toward Shuangqing. There are many lonely officials, sons of harlots, working men, and worried women, who exist in this dusty, hot, malaria-infested place. If they have someone praising them, there are bound to be a hundred defaming them. If they smile, they'll be suspected; if they cry, they'll be blamed. When people meet them, they dislike their looks; when they turn to go, people even dislike their backs. What has happened, though, is that Heaven has heaped all this onto the one person of Shuangqing!"

Mengzhan's bondmaid brought two orchids from Shuangqing. On them was written her poem, "Willow Catkins" (柳絮):

> The willow catkins with sentiment
> Have become like duckweeds;
> Their pure spirit, drifts quietly
> In the current of fallen petals.
> Listen! Are those swallows
> Chattering at third watch?
> Sailing over the top of the flowering tree,
> The moon darkens again.
>
> 柳絮多情已化萍，素魂紅怨淡無聲。
> 似聞燕子三更語，月過花梢又不明。

Anshu adorned himself with the orchids. They gradually faded and the verse was lost. So he walked around aimlessly with his brow knitted, holding onto the letter from Shuangqing and muttering the line, "A single word from the immortal is greater than an ever-luminescent pearl." He wanted to die over it.

Mengzhan's bondmaid reported this to Shuangqing and laughed at her. Shuangqing told her, "He has misinterpreted me. 'Immortal' refers to my husband. My husband does not read. I teach him under the lamp, and now he knows ten or more words. Other people may know ten thousand words, but that is nothing great. When my husband learns one word, I am truly elated. That is why I call it an ever-luminescent pearl. I don't need to admire the scholar-official, Xu Ling 徐陵 of Southern Dynasties. My husband could not write. I have held his hand and helped him trace some lines and dots. I am not thinking of the great calligrapher-painter, Wang Xizhi 王羲之 ."

She therefore wrote a letter to Anshu to explain herself. [Translator's note: In this letter He Shuangqing demonstrated the depth of her scholarship by using a defunct, though exquisite, ancient style of writing in which sentences run in couplets and many literary allusions are used. It can only be appreciated in the original; any attempt to translate it would only do it disservice. The general meaning, though, is this: He Shuangqing's aim in this letter was to correct Anshu's misunderstanding of her line in the letter. She started by describing the scenic environment of Xiaoshan to reflect on her inner emotions. Then she went into her life and her fragile health to say how she strove to perform her many household duties. She told Anshu of her affectionate relationship with her husband and implied from that that it was her intention to treasure her marriage with no desire to become a great writer and calligrapher on her own.]

I left Xiaoshan on the seventeenth day. A couple of days later Mengzhan went to visit a friend at Wuxi 無錫 . He plans to go boating on East Lake and to call on Anshu to dissuade him from worrying over Shuangqing.

Scholar Shen Zhilun

Shen Zhilun 申志綸 is a native of Beijing. His father, who is an official in Jintan, is honest and kind. Zhilun follows his father around the country on the latter's official rounds and is educated by him. He is very studious and seldom ventures from home. On one occasion he found in a bookstore many books he had not read. These he wanted to buy with all the money he had with him, but that being insufficient, he took off his jacket as collateral. Once he dreamed he was in a garden where there was a huge library full of books unknown to this world. The library bore the name of "The Drunken Scholar Immortal" (醉書仙). When he woke up, he adopted this as his pen name. Open and lofty in outlook, he regards power and money with disdain. When he meets up with people who worship names, he avoids them saying laughingly, "They are like ants—heartless. I'll find my bosom friends through books." When Li Yunchou 李雲綢 [42] showed him the story of He Shuangqing, Shen said with feeling, "Now The Drunken Scholar Immortal will never wake up again." He responded to Shuangqing's poetry, writing forty-four verses and six essays entitled: "Aspiring for a Meeting," "Drafting a Letter," "Empty Questions," "Easing My Roar of Lamentation," "Sweeping Away the Mist" and "Greeting Spring."

Shen's preface for these essays reads:

> How suddenly emotions strike! They spread arterially and deepen quietly. Once you tug at their terminals, you become entangled with them. When human beings grieve, does the Creator grieve also? Shuangqing with her beauty, talent and suffering, is now recorded in Shi Zhenlin's *Sanji*. When The Drunken Scholar Immortal reads about her, he feels as if he is drunk, as if he is another person, as if he is experiencing a dream. When he reads her poetry he responds in verse but cannot express himself fully. For this reason he writes six essays to release his feelings.
>
> With a meeting that cannot be effected, a letter that cannot fully express my feelings, there are questions that cannot be answered, I can only roar my lamentation and try to sweep away the mist in order to see her spring-like countenance. Why? These emotions are in a myriad of strands. When I put them in order, other emotions will appear in disarray. When I ask other people about this, they cannot help me. When I ask the Creator, the Creator has no answer. That is why I am writing this to ask Shi Zhenlin.

His "Drafting a Letter" reads, in brief:

> I am lost, unhappy. I cannot find the herb to help Shuangqing forget her sorrows. I cannot compound the right medicine for her sickness. Therefore, I send Shuangqing this letter:
>
> "By chance I write a poem in sympathy with your untold suffering. In the lines of 'There is a swarm of crows gathered in the tree at

twilight, / Yet it is the lean crane that stands out on the bank,' is the crane you?

"And yet the Creator's love for talent cannot be without some purpose. If he should have hidden you in some rich household, your every move would have been given protection and solicitude. Then you would be like an unfeeling plant, you would have disappeared into the mist. Instead, the Creator uses every way possible to sculpt your beauty and cultivate your intelligence, limiting them only by your fate. Heaven develops your gift of talent; that alone makes your life worthwhile. As a scholar, I don't let myself succumb to beauty but I cannot ignore talent. I have responded to your poetry. I hope you will take care of yourself and not be overcome by grief."

His "Easing My Roar of Lamentation" is excerpted as follows:

The Drunken Scholar Immortal told Li Yunchou, "I have seen Shuangqing. Not only have I seen her, but I have also cried for her." Yunchou said, "You are lying to me." The Drunken Scholar Immortal replied, "In her lyrics on the chrysanthemum and the wild goose, I see her simple, tranquil environment; in her image of 'moonlight of shaved ice,' I imagine her free and bright disposition; in her references to 'hungry swallow' and 'sick silkworms' I feel her compassionate nature; in her brilliant mind and her sympathy for flowers, I see her keen talent."

Yunchou said, "Then why do you cry?" The Drunken Scholar Immortal said, "The broken sword is now thrown into the water; the dying pine lies in the precipice; I cry for Shuangqing's fate. A beautiful flower is under torrential rain; the new moon is hidden in the clouds; I cry for her beauty. The pearl cannot raise itself from the deep water; the jade cannot lift itself from the jade stone; I cry for Shuangqing's talent. The plum can stand the snow; the chrysanthemum savors light frost; I cry for her virtue."

His "Sweeping Away the Mist" is summarized thus:

There is a Mr. "Bookhamper" who on perceiving The Drunken Scholar Immortal responding to Shuangqing's poetry, rolled his eyes in

> anger. He said, "You cannot do that. For the two sexes to be singing and responding to each other violates decorum. Destroy what you have written, don't foul the written language invented by Master Cangjie 倉頡 ."[43]
>
> The Drunken Scholar Immortal leaned against the table, smiled and said, "The ancients guarded themselves from falling for beautiful women, but were never prohibited from loving talent. Whenever they met talent, they appreciated it. Why should you differentiate between male and female? You may say this is sexual attraction, actually it is Dao. Cangjie hates you, don't you know? With great inspiration and creativity, he worked hard at inventing the language only to have people who came after him use his writing to make lackluster essays. Now Shuangqing uses it with her heaven-given talent; The Drunken Scholar Immortal uses it to encourage talent. You are obstructing all this by throwing a wet blanket over it. If Cangjie knew about this, he would weep in the night, whether he is a ghost or not."

His essays, "Aspiring for a Meeting," "Empty Questions," and "Greeting Spring" were all sad but direct. He was not yet thirty but had already written much poetry and prose. He came to look me up three times but missed me every time. I then wrote him. One day we met in the lane and have since become good friends.

Scholar Jing Zhenxiang and Zhang Tianshen

Jing Zhenxiang 荊振翔 has his studio two *li* southeast of Ganlu Shrine (甘露菴). His father, Jing Lingyun 荊凌雲 studied at Tushan 圖山 , where the Lingbo Immortal (淩波仙女) came to him through divination and requested that he record her story. It became a drama called *The Huaniao yuan* 花鳥緣 (The Romance of the Flowers and the Birds). He gave a feast and invited the immortals residing in Tushan, serving them tea and fruits on ten or more tables. During the festival strange happenings, like goblets lifting themselves into the air, stirred up much commotion in that mountain community.

In the fourth month that summer, Jing Zhenxiang and Xiao Dongyuan 綃東垣 came to Xiaoshan for a visit. When Jing returned from that trip, he became depressed and lost his appetite. During the day he copied my *Xiqing sanji*, at night he read Shuangqing's poetry. He had insomnia. He took walks among the bamboo that proliferate in this area and chose young bamboos on which to carve Shuangqing's poetry with his side-arm sword. This he did all over the grove. He said, "The bamboo has impeccable looks and character. Its feelings are like the spirit of the orchid. It is appropriate to present it with words of a lady who is peerless in this world."

He told me that when he was twenty, he was still in a fog. At that time, he said, he did not enjoy literature or poetry. Then he came across Shuangqing's poetry and it made a new person out of him. He said he felt that since creation the laments and depressions in the world make life joyless and death meaningless, and, yet, he felt a person must have a soul the way a body has a shadow. When he was directionless, he used poetry to overcome his insomnia.

I replied, "Unless a person is extremely stupid, he must have some talent. The question is how to bring out that talent. It's like the scent in a piece of wood, only heat will bring it out. Like a seed, it needs moisture to sprout. Young people who are lazy and unintelligent are not necessarily lacking in scent or seeds. The fault could lie in the method used to heat or moisten them. At the same time, if a piece of scented wood is left unheated, it rots; if a seed stays unmoistened, it decays. Then too, if you should reverse the method of treatment by using moisture to bring out the scent of the wood or planting the seed in fire, that will destroy any chance for the scent of wood to emerge or the seed to sprout. Furthermore, the way talent is used is also important. If the scent is confined to the toilet and the sprout is fed to the animals, they are wasted."

During my stay at Ganlu Shrine, Jing Zhenxiang used to come visit me morning and night. Well-dressed and carrying a circular fan, he had a distinctive air about him. The weather was hot, but he was always impeccably dressed and somehow stayed cool. He wrote two poems on Xiaoshan, one while touring the place and the other at his departure.

The master of Ganlu Shrine is a farmer named Zhang Tianshen 張天申 . He is honest and without guile. He enjoys the simple pleasures in his farm. He has compassion for all animate life, and his family has abstained from meat and wine for five or six generations.[44] Living like a hermit, he farms contentedly. He does not engage in profit-making pursuits. His seventy-year-old mother once prepared some vegetarian fare for me and asked me about my *Xiqing sanji* and my records on Shuangqing. Though illiterate, Tianshen knows enough to encourage his daughter to listen from behind the screen whenever Jing Zhenxiang reads Shuangqing's poetry aloud, for he wants her to emulate Shuangqing. He tells Jing that his daughter has wept over Shuangqing many times.

At the end of the seventh month, Chi'an plans to ask Jing Zhenxiang to bring his scroll on Mount Qixia (棲霞山)[45] to show Shuangqing in Xiaoshan and to ask her for some poetry on autumn lotus written with pollen on autumn leaves. In the meantime, Keshan 柯山 [46] is going south to bid farewell to Anshu, for he wants to bring my *Xiqing sanji* manuscript north across the Yellow River to Mount Tai (泰山)[47] to visit the tomb of Confucius. He also wants to go to Yantai (燕台) with the hope of meeting some extraordinary persons from the hermits and the officials.

On the twenty-first day of the seventh month, Jing came to say goodbye. He was bringing his "Ten Poems on the Autumn Lotus" to Shuangqing for her to harmonize. He said to me, "People who suspect Shuangqing's existence always find it hard to believe that a farmer's daughter can be literate and can also write. Nor can they understand how she can write so well. They are further surprised that she has intoxicated Duan Yuhan, startled Anshu, conquered Ningxi, and made them forget their hunger and thirst and even acquire a touch of madness, crying and laughing. How come all this dizziness?" So he left.

Last Poems from He Shuangqing

On the evening of the twenty-fourth, Bi Keshan talked with me in a bamboo grove. He said, "Shuangqing is poverty-stricken, yet patient; she is like a dying fish on a string. She cannot cry out for help even if she were near water. I am going north to collect funds from some scholars for the printing of your *Sanji* so that Shuangqing can become an example for other ill-starred persons. When I come south again, I shall give her husband some money to build a pavilion to be called 'The Bring-lunch Pavilion,' as well as money to buy some land to plant melons and to dig a pond for her to wash clothes." I laughed, saying, "You are so generous. You'd give up all you have for a cause. Now empty-handedly you want to be a fund raiser. I'm afraid your tongue is not eloquent enough to bring in any money."

On the twenty-eighth day, Chi'an gave a farewell dinner for Keshan. I was sick and could not attend. Jing Zhenxiang came from Xiaoshan with Shuangqing's "Ten Poems on the Autumn Lotus" (秋荷十首) written on tea rose leaves. With each branch having five leaves, there is a poem written on each leave. The leaves are small and so the characters are mere shadows. Her poems read:

I.

I receive no communications,
Even the crickets cry for me;
My heart is like the rolled plantain leaf
Still to loosen.
The chrysanthemum can stand frost,
Though the frost tries to be kind.
It is at its peak of bloom,
While the plum has yet to come into its own.

錦鱗無信泣秋蛩，心似芭蕉卷未鬆。
幽性耐霜霜不忍，梅花猶淡菊花濃。

II.

The chrysanthemum and the plum
Both know their own time.
At sunset the farmhands leave,
The egrets return.
Does the immortal care to sacrifice
To the goddess of flowers?
Let him also offer
At the shrine of grievous women.

菊意梅魂兩自知，夕陽人去鷺回時。
仙郎肯祭花神否？願配人間怨女祠。

III.

The lady's grievance is cooled
By the morning breeze;
Dew drops on lotus leaves,
While little fish watch quietly.
The lotus seed harbors a heart
That turns bitter in autumn;
Where but the moon
Can you place your tenderness?

女郎清怨曉涼吹，露滴魚兒冷眼窺。
蓮子有心秋正苦，不憐明月更憐誰？

IV.

Moonlight is as cold as water,
All the butterflies have vanished.
The moon's feeble light weakens;
The land becomes cold, desolate.
Night rain resumes,
Shattering the petals;
The mermaids, on meeting,
Will be drained of tears.[48]

月明如水蝶全無，微豔初消凜凜孤。
夜雨又來紅欲碎，鮫人相見淚應枯。

V.

Tears exhausted,
The mermaids have no desire to shed pearls.
What retribution from my last life
I can only guess at in this.
I sent a branch of lotus away,[49]
Severing its milky strands;
In the seventh month
The wild geese are returning early this year.

淚盡鮫珠不願開，前生香孽此生猜。
一枝遠寄千絲斷，七月江南雁早來。

VI.

The sunset silhouettes the early wild geese;
The moon, the person.
The water chestnut is aggressive,
The lotus is impoverished.
Does the yellow bird ever

Take pity on the white bird?
Now, unlike spring,
Flowers in the wild pond are unprized.

霞邊新雁月邊人，菱芡爭欺菡萏貧。
黃鳥可知憐白鳥，野塘花賤不如春。

VII.

The autumn lotus demurely views
Its thin reflection in the pond.
The current's sway
Allows it little peace at night.
Its leaves screen off the blustering rain;
Its flowers, the frost;
Tenderly it protects the mandarin ducks
Even when their dreams may be chilled.

淡影羞春鏡裏看，水心搖曳夜難安。
葉遮猛雨花遮露，香護鴛鴦夢可寒。

VIII.

The love-sick mandarin drake is dreamless,
Enjoying his prime.
My weary feeling began
Before the autumn moon and cassia bloom.
Having to mend the many colored flowers
Around West Lake,
Will this grieve
The heart of Nüwa?[50]

癡鴛無夢攬芳年，愁在銀蟾桂子先。
補遍西湖花五色，傷心可是女媧天？

IX.

The colorful horizon
Ushers in a lonely dusk.

I use my tears to grind autumn pollen
For sketching in the moonlight.
Carefully I pick up
Every lotus petal and lightly grind,
Then shape it into pellets
To scent my curtained bed.

五色天邊寂寞宵，淚研秋粉月中描。
細收花片輕輕碾，搓就香丸帳裏燒。

X.

The scented pellets are burnt,
Giving off blue smoke.
The chanced union of two people—
A fate how deceiving!
From now on since I can't
Be separated from you,
I'll cut up remnants
To mend your coir cloak.

香丸燒盡碧烟多，萍水因緣簿豈訛？
從此並頭分不得，裂紅裁翠補漁簑。

Keshan said, "I traveled a thousand *li* to this place and now I have obtained your *Xiqing sanji* and Shuangqing's poems on the lotus. I have bagged both the scholar and the beauty. When I take them over the Yellow River, won't these treasures rival those of the Dragon King!"[51]

I returned to Jintan and continued to have dysentery. Mengzhan welcomed me to rest at Xiaoshan again. Shuangqing wrote nine verses on autumn for me containing these lines:

The cicada, cold and hungry,
Clings to the withered mulberry leaf;
The sick butterfly flying low,

Looks for old leek flowers.
Life and death are so hazy
One forgets one's age;
Happiness and sorrow recall
Clearly the passage of time.

In the eleventh month of that year I got better and so returned to Guazhu, where I recovered completely in the following month. Anshu wrote to invite me to Jishan 姬山 . He and I spent New Year's Eve there and enjoyed the lantern festival at Piling 毗陵 . We stayed at the Bell Tower Temple (鐘樓寺). My absence from home at this time caused me to miss an invitation from Jin Baiyan 金白岩 to go to his Wanyi yuan 晚宜園 estate as an editor [see pp. 134–35]. This invitation was declined for me by my uncle since I was not home. When I left Anshu on the tenth day of the second month in 1735 and got to Jintan, I received two poems from Shuangqing, "Plum Blossoms" and "Bringing Lunch to the Field," both written to the tune of *Chun cong tianshang lai* 春從天上來 . A few days later Anshu again welcomed me to the Bell Tower Temple. When he read these poems, he was saddened.

Many women at Piling were acquainted with Shuangqing's work. They constantly besieged me for her poetry through messengers. I also sent her poetry to many others.

During the intercalary[52] fourth month Nazhai came. He and I left Anshu to go south to Benniu zhen 奔牛鎮 , lodging at Sanli Shrine. We visited Chen Xingye 陳星野 at Lücheng, then went north to Xiejia wan 謝家灣 and stayed at Ningxi's studio for ten days. There each of us wrote ten or more pieces of poetry. When people came for my calligraphy, I used poems written by Ningxi and Nazhai in response. It was then that I regretted that Cao Zhenting did not have a chance to meet Shuangqing.

I left Xiaoshan in 1733. In the summer of 1734 I made a trip to Menghe and in the following spring went to Lanling 蘭陵 [i.e.,

Piling]. I heard that Shuangqing became ever so careful in serving her mother-in-law, and her neighbors all praise her for being filial. Her husband's temper grew worse, but Shuangqing saw to it that he was well taken care of. She labored throughout the year. Her unused books and brushes have been put away in a torn basket, and she dared not even steal a look at them. As a matter of fact, she hardly had time to do so.

On New Year's Eve Shuangqing was reading the *Lengyan jing* by the lamp of the stove when her mother-in-law came home. Upon seeing this, the old woman seized the book and scolded, "Half a book of torn papers! If a *xiucai* 秀才 [53] should pay attention to this type of stuff, he would surely starve to death! You stupid, are you thinking of taking the 'women's examination?'" At another time Shuangqing was washing her inkstone when her husband balked, "Are you trying to get away from work by playing with a piece of clay? Even soot scraped from a cauldron is more useful than ink, at least it furnishes some fertilizer for the field!"

Shuangqing's calligraphy had dignified beauty, but she never kept any because she used the paper she wrote on to start the fire for cooking. She also kept daily accounts for her husband's wine making. Sometimes her illiterate husband looked askance at these records to say abusively, "This character is upside down," but Shuangqing usually smiled when she told him, "No."

Shuangqing's poem on the plum blossoms (梅花) written to the tune of *Chun cong tianshang lai* reads:

> Placidly I laugh at myself,
> Taking time from the busy season of spring
> To examine the tips of your petals.
> You look languid—
> I wonder for whom you multiply.
> Since my illness,
> I share the regret with flowers.

The winter clothes demand washing—
Spring water is cold,
Immersing my wrists I dread.
The east wind is harsh;
In vain have you been fragrant during winter.
The new moon is slim.

Kind Heaven pollinates you.
This only beguiles me
To seek my fortune in my dreams,
To help the butterfly call back her soul,[54]
To wipe away the tears for the oriole.
In the middle of the night
Stealthily I read the *Lengyan jing*.
In it I found a beautiful line regretting spring:
"Whether sad or bitter,
Life, death are both sweet."
I pray a happy year for you;
I bow my head to the Goddess of Mercy,
I've consulted every bamboo slip[55] in the lot.

自笑懨懨，費半晌春忙，去省花尖。玉容憔悴，知爲誰添？病來分與花嫌。正臘衣催洗，春波冷，素腕愁沾。硬東風，枉寒香一度，新月纖纖。　　多情滿天墜粉，偏只累雙卿，夢裏空拈，與蝶招魂，替鶯拭淚，夜深偷誦楞嚴，有傷春佳句：酸和苦，生死俱甜。祝花年，向觀音稽首，掣徧靈籤。

Her poem, "Bringing Lunch to the Field" (餉耕) written to the same tune of *Chun cong tianshang lai* reads:

The purple path is alive with spring,
I cover my forehead with a light spring scarf,
Set out to bring lunch to the spring planting.
The small plum is spring-thin in blossoms;
The fine grass is spring-radiant;
Every step in the spring field is resplendent with spring growth.
I recall the year when spring was beautiful,

I told my spring emotions to the spring swallow.
As for now,
When I think of spring poems, spring tears,
They have all become spring ice to me.

How many springs have I felt tenderly toward spring, loved spring?
A layer of spring mist
Cages the spring oriole—
Let me make a gift of it to you, Spring;
I'll hand it to you, Spring.
This is me, the same as your spring spirit.
I can count your spring beginnings and spring endings,
But I can't count all the spring dreams, spring awakenings you've evoked.
What spring demon brings
This spring illness for the spring?
Spring, you've deceived me!

紫陌春晴，慢額裹春紗，自餉春耕。小梅春瘦，細草春明，春田步步春生。記那年春好，向春燕、說破春情。到於今，想春箋春淚，都化春冰。　　憐春痛春春幾？被一片春烟，鎖住春鶯，贈與春儂，遮將春你，是儂是你春靈。算春頭春尾，也難算春夢春醒。甚春魔？做一春春病。春誤雙卿！

In the fourth month the wild roses bloomed profusely by the roadside, both the pink and the white varieties. If your hand happened to brush against them, you carry their fragrance with you throughout the day. Even when she was occupied with threshing wheat, Shuangqing worried over the petals of these roses falling. Sometimes she cradled their fallen petals in her arms to either bury them under her window or piece them into characters on her pillow when she took a nap. When she sprinkled water on the clay floor to gather the dust for sweeping, she scattered the rose petals in front of her bed, then she walked in between them, laughing and crying. This made her husband angry. He told her, "People who destroy flowers will become ugly in their next life. You are not good-looking in this life, but you still want to destroy flowers?"

Shuangqing loved cleanliness. Although she lived in a humble home, she always kept her hair neat and clean. In contrast, her husband had body odor and the accumulation of dirt on his neck was quite visible. He objected violently whenever Shuangqing pleaded with him to take a bath, and so she refrained from her entreaty. She asked the artist Shilin to paint the white robed goddess for her. In the deep of night, she worshipped the goddess in front of this painting with an offering of fresh water. But again, her husband liked to harass her, saying, "What is all this you are trying to attain? Isn't marrying me enough of a blessing?" Although Shuangqing was not sick at this time, such abusive remarks depressed her spirit and caused her to lose weight. She told her friend, Han Xi, "I taste bitterness in my mouth, especially when I eat sweets. I wonder why?"

In 1736, Chen San 陳三, about fifty years old, worked as the doorman for Yu Daiyuan 于待園, at the provincial capital. No one ever bothered to ask him for his real name; they simply called him Chen the Third [a name that denotes his being the third son in his family]. The first month of that year when I went to Jiangdu 江都 [Yangzhou 揚州] with Yu Daiyuan's elder brother, Yu Nansha 于南沙, we found this doorman very polite and scholarly. We asked him for his name, and he hesitantly replied, "Chen the Third." He did not dare give us his real name, which is Yiwen 逸文. When Yu Daiyuan was in charge of the imperial examination in the province of Shaanxi 陜西 in 1735, Chen the Third never asked for any gratuity from the scholars who came through the door [to pay their respects to the chief examiner after having passed the examination]. He showed them in whether they gave him money or not, yet for this reason they all laughed at him.

One evening I was reading my *Xiqing sanji* aloud. Chen the Third, who was listening, felt so moved that he said, "A pity that I was not born a woman. Shuangqing is ill-fated but most talented. She has hidden virtue and fame. Very likely people sing her poetry and cry over her because she is a woman. If I were a woman, I might not be as virtuous as she, but I wouldn't make myself so invisible either." I asked him what he is good at. He told me he writes poetry and showed me some of his work.

Written on the Way to the North for the Imperial Examination

In 1735 on the twenty-seventh day of the twelfth month, Yu Nansha and I went to Yangzhou. Cao Zhenting joined us that day. On the second day of the first month in 1736 Zhenting took the government carriage provided for the candidates to go north and agreed to wait for us at Huai 淮. We started on the fifth, but upon reaching Huai, Zhenting had already left for Tai'anzhou 泰安州 to visit Mount Tai and left a message that he would wait for us there.

I wrote nine verses harmonizing some of Shuangqing's poetry.

Liu Mengchuan 劉孟川 of Piling, with whom Zhenting passed the provincial examination, came to Jiangdu with some of Shuangqing's poetry. Another scholar by the name of Li Yuzhong 李餘中 of Yizheng 儀徵 who is talented, knowledgeable and filial, was one of the passengers in a government carriage. Everyone in Jiangdu tried to persuade him to stop over but he, being a filial son, declined on account of his mother's warning about Jiangdu [Jiangdu or Yangzhou was known as a sinful city at that time]. He was in the same carriage as Cheng Jiexuan 程接軒. We all met at the foot of Mount Tai. In the carriage he wrote more than ten poems. There was one for Shuangqing with these lines, "You have great love for the language; / You stay chaste and pure. / Preserve the air of *The Odes*, / Censor that from Zheng and Wei."[56]

Zhenting told me, "Since I saw you last, I have met many pure-hearted scholars. However, they all think I am boasting about Shuangqing. None of them believes there could be a person in the world like her." He wrote nine poems using the rhyme of his old poem "Autumn" about Shuangqing.

Wu Zhensheng 吳震生 is twenty years old and calls himself "The Old Widower" 鰥叟 after the death of his beloved wife, and his pen name is the "Yugou Lyric Poet" (玉勾詞客). He has great admiration for Shuangqing's character. He regrets that his wife, a poet in her own right, is dead. He thinks that if she were alive, she would personally go to Xiaoshan to pay her respects to Shuangqing and welcome her to their studios. He is of the opinion that the sympathy women have for each other is more intense than that between men. He observed that if Shuangqing were a man, even though there may be rich gentlemen who sympathized with her, still they would not be able to rescue her from her poverty and dire straits. He said, "If Shuangqing were a man, she and her admirer may be well matched physically, but may not agree emotionally. If they agree emotionally, there is still the question of their being united in spirit." He thought that if his deceased wife could have seen Shuangqing, she would dry Shuangqing's tears for her, comfort and assure her with the zeal of a person who loves talent.

Yugou wrote two poems, one of which was done in fancy allusions to praise Shuangqing's talent and to vow his help in spreading her name. The other marveled at Shuangqing's ability to endure her bleak farm life and to be a poet at the same time. Zhenting agreed with him, adding, "For example, in eating honey, both the inside and the outside are sweet. In Shuangqing's case though, the inside is sweet, but the outside is somewhat bitter."

"Yugou Lyric Poet" commented, "Still, it is better than to have the outside sweet and the inside bitter."

The Daughters of Jin Baiyan

Jin Baiyan of Maochuan 茅川 owned the country estate, Wanyi yuan. Wealthy, he and his family lived quietly west of the Fuluo Mountain (佛螺山). He had no son, and only one daughter by the second of his four secondary wives. Named Wanjuan 晚娟 , the daughter was beautiful and intelligent. She was brought up to worship the Goddess of Mercy and was instilled with filial piety. The family called her the Jade Moon Goddess. When she was born, her father was already fifty years old. Wanjuan was studious and preferred a quiet life. Accordingly, her father built an attached studio for her in a secluded bamboo area of his estate and selected four bright looking maids as her attendants to serve her. Once during her father's illness, she prayed to the Goddess of Mercy and refrained from sleep for over a month [as an act of penance]. She wrote a prayer with her own blood and burned it as a petition to the goddess on her father's behalf. When the prayer was being offered in the ritual, a strong fragrance permeated her father's bed. Instantly he was cured. Since then the family also calls her the Goddess of Mercy.

One hundred servants were employed to take care of the vast estate. Everyday, visitors by the score came; they joked and drank in the garden. Wanjuan pleaded with her father, saying, "These visitors are not worthy people. If they are poor and need help, simply bestow alms on them so that they may devote themselves to some productive livelihood. I'm afraid all this gathering leads nowhere." She further counseled him, saying, "Father, you love entertaining so much that you have spent half your life bowing complaisantly to passersby, thus allowing yourself no peace. The overbearing visitors talk extravagantly; the timid ones are reserved; the wise keep quiet; only the small minds brag about themselves. Often a job fails even when you employ one hundred people, and yet if you used but one right man, the job gets done. It's a matter of knowing how to choose the good from the bad. I wish you, my father, not to labor yourself on account of these visitors." Her father took her advice and stopped entertaining idle visitors. He sent away the more handsome of his servants and kept only the old and the young ones in his service. The house quieted down to become not unlike the abode of a poor scholar. After a couple of weeks, he said, "Now I am beginning to appreciate the joy of peaceful living."

In 1734, when he reached sixty-six, he bought a girl from the Ye family of West Lake for one thousand pieces of gold as another concubine. She looks so much like Wanjuan that when she first arrived, the family was astonished at their resemblance and started calling her by Wanjuan's pet name, the Jade Moon Goddess. Wanjuan sent her wet nurse to invite the bride to meet her. After this she went to see her father. She wept and told him that in a dream the Goddess of Mercy had told her, "Your younger sister will be coming." Immediately she set up a sacrifice before the goddess and swore an oath with the bride as her younger sister, saying, "I have now appropriated you." When her father heard about what she had done, he smiled and said, "Here I've been hoping for a boy, but I've gained another daughter!" So the bride became his adopted daughter and was given the name of Yijuan 宜娟.

In 1735 Baiyan sent a messenger to Jintan inviting me to go to his estate to edit some poetry. At that time I was with Anshu in Lanling and so could not accept the invitation. There are only a few scholars at Maochuan where Jin's estate is located, because the inhabitants of that area are mostly farmers and merchants.

Through the years, scholars, who visited Wanyi yuan, have written a thousand poems for Jin. Many of them introduced themselves this way with the hope of being picked as the son-in-law. A known poet himself, Baiyan wrote a preface and wanted to have the poems edited and published. He selected five poems by a young man as being superior. The young man was from a rich family and Jin had his eyes on him as the future son-in-law. On hearing about this, Wanjuan sniffled and told Yijuan, "Talent with sensitivity reflects the living spirit of heaven and earth and is the very soul of men. But beautiful writing can come from the mouth of some stupid people; this is the worst of calamities. I'm afraid Wanyi yuan will be plundered soon."

Yijuan plays the flute and is knowledgeable about music. The two girls love each other like sisters. They dress alike and even use similar accessories. Wanjuan shares her own maid attendants with Yijuan. In the quiet of the night they enjoy walking hand in hand under the moonlight, while their attendants brew fine tea for them in the shadow of the flowers. Their low conversation is often accompanied by sighs. Yijuan owns a famous flute. This she plays with great feeling, leading Wanjuan's wet nurse to muse, "The two of you should be married to the same person!" Whereupon the girls had a Goddess of Mercy carved from a piece of red jade and encased it in crystal for worship. In front of the goddess they swore that they would not part in life or death. Baiyan addressed the two girls as Juan-Juan and they usually responded together.

On the seventh month of that year Jin died. I was taking my [provincial] examination in Jinling 金陵 [Nanjing] and happened to pass north of Fuluo Mountain, thirty *li* from Jin's estate. At a teahouse I rested and asked the hostess about the Jin family. She knows them well, because she is the elder sister of Wanjuan's wet nurse. She told me that since the Jin's have no dependable relatives, matchmakers have been pouring into the estate with exaggerated claims of their candidates' qualification. In the meantime, she said, Jin's coffin is still awaiting burial. She further stated that his daughters are guarding it day and night, crying all the time, and besides, Yijuan has fallen sick.

My inability to accept Jin's invitation was regretted by Zhao Fengqi 趙鳳岐,[57] Chao Nazhai and Jing Zhenxiang. The imperial examination was held in 1736, after which we remained in the capital. In the beginning of the sixth month "Yugou Lyric Poet" dreaded the heat on account of his health and so arranged with us to spend the summer in the western hills. When we talked about what was happening to the Jin family, it made Zhenting unhappy. He was worried that since Jin is dead, Jin's two daughters will fall into the hands of the poisonous matchmakers, exactly as Shuangqing did. "Yugou Lyric Poet" wrote a poem lamenting the likely breakup of the two sisters amidst the collapse of their family. When my *Xiqing sanji* is published, I must send the first copy to Jin's estate so that his daughters will learn from Shuangqing's experience and not be ruined by the matchmakers.

[Translator's note: The record of He Shuangqing in Shi Zhenlin's *Xiqing sanji* ended with this note of anguish from the scholars. Their concern for He Shuangqing had now broadened to include other women destined to meet the same fate. Through the few years that they had known He Shuangqing, the scholars witnessed her struggle with, and final transcendence over, the difficult conditions of her life. They now saw the same fatal peril coming to other lives. He Shuangqing had wanted her work, which mapped her own steps, to serve as an example for other people in the same predicament "not to blame themselves but to value poetry and education and practice propriety in order to keep themselves chaste for the sake of their parents and the future generations" (p. 90). The scholars, though, were now in the capital after the imperial examination. It was not until two years later that they returned south. By that time He Shuangqing had passed away. Then in fulfillment, perhaps, of her hope that her work be shared, Shi Zhenlin with the help of the "Yugou Lyric Poet" (that is, Wu Zhensheng) published the *Xiqing sanji* in 1738.

We do not have a record of whether Shi Zhenlin sent a copy of his *Xiqing sanji* to the daughters of Jin Baiyan or of what happened to them. Nevertheless, the sisters' impending difficulties, which probably would be similar to He Shuangqing's, would be yet another disillusionment that hastened Shi Zhenlin into retirement seven years later, seeking salvation with his Buddhist friends.]

Notes

1. *Xin jing* 心經 (Heart sutra): see note 42 in "The Poet and Her Chronicler."
2. Bailuo 白羅 was one of the female immortals conjured up by the scholars through divination. See *Xiqing sanji*, p. 2. For divination, see note 2 in "The Poet and Her Chronicler."
3. The western mountains (西山) referred to here is thought to be the generally mountainous region west of Xiaoshan, Jintan, as there is no specific mountain called Western Hill or Mountain in this area.
4. The Toad on the moon is a folklore belief that there is a toad living in the moon.
5. In Chinese legend the carp sometimes transforms itself into a dragon whose ascent into heaven brings thunder and, therefore, rain, an act beneficial to farming. There are also various stories of a carp appearing in a dream as a person dressed in shiny armor (like scales) or colored clothes (according to the type of carp), pleading for the dreamer to save its life. When the dreamer woke up, he would find a carp near death and so release it in the river. The carp would come into his dream again to thank him for his good deed. See *Gujin tushu jicheng* 古今圖書集成 (The Encyclopedia of Chinese Works from Early Times to the Present) (Shanghai: Zhonghua shuju, 1934), *han* 57, vol. 526, *juan* 139, pp. 15–17. See reference in note 10 in "The Poet and Her Chronicler."
6. Wang Danyuan 王澹園 was a scholar of lofty ideals, well meaning and Confucian in outlook, whom Shi Zhenlin sometimes addressed as Master (先生) because of his age. They were actually fellow students under Master Zhang Xiuyuan's 張修圓 tutorage in Xiaoshan in 1733 (see p. 64). A poor, peaceful and contented soul, Wang was Shi's companion in much of his travels, such as the trip visiting scholar friends in Menghe in 1733. In the beginning, his Confucian reserve made him frown on He Shuangqing's communications with the other scholars, but this was dissolved by Shi Zhenlin's making up a story about Shuangqing respecting Danyuan for the latter's poetry (see p. 72).

7. Biye 碧夜 was an immortal conjured up through divination by Shi Zhenlin's friend, Lu Xishan 吕習山. She was asked about the heavenly world found through the Cave of Huayang (a Daoist concept and the name of Shi Zhenlin's second journal, *Huayang sangao* or *Huayang Essays*) in the Mao Mountain. She described it as being a huge Daoist shrine with five gates to the outer world and connected directly to the sacred peaks in different parts of China. Within the shrine are palaces, one for men and two for women. She further said that the women occupants were those who had already achieved the Dao (the Way), and they held to a magical state that kept them youthful and beautiful despite the passage of time, while they cultivated immortality. She also explained that of the nearly two hundred occupants at that time, most of the women had died either as martyrs or as virtuous women who preserved their chastity above all else. For details see *Xiqing sanji*, p. 57.
8. "Much old sorrow I still owe" is an allusion to the Buddhist belief of karma that a good life is the reward of good deeds from one's past life, and that debts unpaid in one's life are to be incurred in one's future life.
9. "Life, whether salty or sour," that is, life in any form.
10. For a Chinese educated in the classical tradition, to write a poem was the natural response to various situations in life; it was commonly used as a medium for social intercourse.
11. Zhao Anshu 趙闇叔, also named Zhao Li 趙笠, was one of the scholars under Master Zhang Xiuyuan's tutorage at Xiaoshan, and, therefore, a member of Zhang Mengzhan's coterie (see p. 64). Anshu was an abandoned character and a poet who stressed simplicity. He favored the four-character ancient style of poetry. Orphaned when young, he was sickly, but made himself into a scholar and poet. He was infatuated by He Shuangqing and her work. Mengzhan recounted part of his life in a letter to He Shuangqing (see pp. 97–98).
12. This refers to the legend about the mother of the human race, Nuwa 女媧, in her effort to save her people from a great flood and a fire which resulted from the toppling of a column holding up the sky. The god of water, having been defeated by the god of fire, committed

suicide by rushing headlong toward that column. Nüwa cultivated five-color stones, melting them into a liquid to mend the sky. She also killed a giant turtle and used its four feet to strengthen the four corners of the sky over the earth. However, her efforts notwithstanding, something remains amiss even today. For the northwestern sky is a little lower and, therefore, the sun, the moon, and the stars all recede toward that direction. In the opposite southeast, the deep hole created by the fall of the column caused the earth to slant toward it, and this resulted in all the rivers and streams of China running toward that direction to form the ocean. See Yuan Ke 袁珂, *Zhongguo gudai shenhua* 中國古代神話 (Old Legends from China) (Shanghai: Commercial Press, 1950), pp. 18–23. Mengzhan used this allusion to say that Shuangqing had ruined the paintings by cutting out her inscriptions, which might have been written on the upper left hand corner (or northwestern direction) and therefore, should be made to mend the paintings by restoring her inscriptions to them.

13. Yin Xiacun 殷霞村 was a poet and scholar, who came to be tutored by Zhang Xiuyuan and became a member of Mengzhan's coterie in Xiaoshan (see p. 64). A nature-loving man, carefree, peaceful, deep and artistic, he was also forgiving in nature; his poetry showed these characteristics. He was Shi Zhenlin's senior by fifteen years but they often exchanged communications in the form of poetry with each other. See *Xiqing sanji*, pp. 49 and 85.
14. Chen Zainan 陳載南 was one of the students under the tutorage of Master Zhang Xiuyuan and a member of Mengzhan's coterie in Xiaoshan (see p. 64). These scholars were concerned over each other's welfare as they enjoyed each other's company. In Chen's case, he, as well as Mengzhan, did their part to persuade Shi Zhenlin to take the provincial examination in 1734, even though it took Master Zhang to push Shi into final action. See *Xiqing sanji*, pp. 174–75.
15. *Li ji* 禮記 or *Book of Rites*, is believed to have been compiled by two cousins, the Elder and the Younger Dai in the second and first centuries B.C. From eighty-five sections of social rites prepared by the Elder Dai from Confucian documents, the Younger Dai reduced them to forty-six sections. Other scholars contributed to the documents until

the end of the second century A.D. when it became known as a *ji* 記 or "records," and not a *jing* 經 or "classic," which applies to an orthodox text directly from Confucius.

16. Shi Zhenlin was a cousin of Mengzhan and Renzhi through their mother, who was a cousin of Shi's father and the first wife of Master Zhang Xiuyuan 張修圓. She died at thirty-eight in 1712 when Mengzhan was only four. See *Xiqing sanji*, pp. 59–60.
17. Xu Yiyu 許逸輿 was a scholar and tutor of the classics, who died in 1733. He was a good friend of Shi Zhenlin. See *Xiqing sanji*, pp. 56–57. Whenever a member of their group died, Shi and his scholar friends would help to educate the surviving son(s). In Xu's case, Xu's wife asked Shi Zhenlin to help her son with the art of calligraphy, and Master Zhang Xiuyuan volunteered to educate the boy.
18. Goddess of Flowers: 花神 *Huashen*. According to *Yueling guangyi* 月令廣義, the Goddess of Flowers was Nüyi 女夷, a disciple of Madam Wei, the calligrapher. Another personage who was honored as the Goddess of Flowers was Huagu 花姑, who was an eighty-year-old Daoist priestess whose face was perpetually youthful and who excelled in growing flowers.
19. In earlier times, pickled vegetables were a basic food made in every farm household in China.
20. The gift mentioned in Zhang Jinglu's edition which I used for my translation was "月藍香縷溫涼木二端" (p. 91). I was unable to understand what these two woods were until I was in Hong Kong to read the proofs and was shown the Gujin shushi 古今書室 edition of *Xiqing sanji*. The gift mentioned in that edition was "月藍香縷溫涼布二端" (*juan* 2, p. 28a), which was some kind of cloth instead of wood, and it agreed perfectly with the measure of length given. The Gujin shushi edition was in four volumes and was in Chinese stitch binding. It was printed by lithographic process in possibly the early twentieth century.
21. Chongyang 重陽 is the ninth day of the ninth month.
22. Suiren 燧人 was a legendary emperor who was supposed to have discovered how to make fire and taught the people to use fire for cooking.

23. Shennong 神農 was the legendary emperor (3rd millennium B.C.) who taught plants and animals husbandry and the art of herbal medicine, using herbs ground by a pestle in a mortar.
24. *Cao* 操 is a composition for the Chinese *qin* 琴 (zither). Usually associated with misfortune, it emphasizes endurance of the misfortune without resorting to violence. It praises one's ability to stay within decorum in face of misfortune, and is, therefore, an appropriate honor for He Shuangqing.
25. *Hu* 斛 is a dry measure that contains 5 *dou* 斗 (Chinese pecks).
26. "Waists are easily bent" refers to bowing in observation of rituals as officials were required to do. Taken broadly, it points to people who are obsequious.
27. *Xiaolian* 孝廉 : same as *juren* 舉人 , was a second degree graduate who had passed the provincial examination in the old Chinese civil service system and who was now qualified for the imperial examination.
28. It was believed that the phoenix perches only in the *wutong* tree. Shuangqing reasoned that using *wutong* wood for cooking deprives the phoenix of its perch; hence her apology.
29. Xiao Qing 小青 , of the Ming dynasty, was named Feng Xuanxuan. She became the concubine of Scholar Feng of Hangzhou. To avoid the taboo of having similar surnames, she simply called herself Xiao Qing. Sensitive to poetry and music, she had to live by herself because Feng's first wife would not tolerate her. One of her relatives, a Mrs. Yang, advised her to remarry, but she would not do so. Resentment and grief made her ill. She had an artist paint her portrait and after offering libation in front of it, died broken-hearted. She was only eighteen at the time. She was buried in Gushan Islet in the West Lake. Mrs. Yang collected her poetry and had it published under the title of *Fengao yu* 焚稿餘 (Remnants of Burnt Manuscripts). Her story was used in a drama during the Ming dynasty.
30. Huayang 華陽 , for its Daoist concept, see note 7 above.
31. The Chinese "cupid" is an old man who binds a couple into a union with a piece of red silk.
32. The Jade Pavilion of Qin refers to the story of King Mu of Qin whose

daughter, who played the flute, admired the skill of the best flute-player in the kingdom. The king consented to their marriage and built for them the Jade Pavilion, where they were happy together. One day they turned themselves into a pair of phoenixes, which are birds that connote conjugal felicity, and flew away toward heaven.

33. *Mu* 畝 is a unit of land measure. It is reckoned as 733.3 sq. yards; thus 6.6 *mu* equal one acre.
34. Yu Erjie 于爾喈, also named Xiaoshan 小山, was a child prodigy. He was a poet whom Shi Zhenlin respected and knew intimately. Their friendship was described by Shi as one "in which all the outward ceremony of physical existence can be ignored" (see *Xiqing sanji*, p. 117).
35. *Li sao* 離騷 (Encountering Sorrow) is a long narrative poem written by the great statesman-poet, Qu Yuan 屈原 (ca. 343–278 B.C.), whose loyalty to the King of Chu remained steadfast through slander and banishment. In his despair he wrote *Li sao*, through whose hauntingly beautiful images, both physical and religious, he reaffirmed his uncompromising uprightness, an ideal which in the end made him drown himself in the Miluo River (汨羅江) rather than follow the political wind of the time. This historical incident is commemorated by the Dragon Boat Festival on the fifth day of the fifth month. For Chu, see note 35 in "The Poet and Her Chronicler."
36. *Nanhua* or the *Nanhua jing* 南華經 is the name given to the works of Zhuangzi, a Daoist philosopher, and was taken from that of a hill in Shandong province where he went into retirement.
37. *Lengyan jing* 楞嚴經 (*Surangama sutra*), translated by Pramiti or Paramiti in A.D. 705, is a large and somewhat shapeless sutra which reveals the causes of illusion leading to existence and how to escape from it. See *A Dictionary of Buddhism, Chinese-Sanskrit-English-Thai* (published by The Chinese Buddhist Order of Sangha in Bangkok, Thailand, 1976; reprinted in Taipei by Tianhua chuban Co., 1982), p. 562.
38. Bianhe 卞和 of Chu found an unpolished jade stone from Mt. Jingshan 荊山. He presented it to the king who suspected it to be a fake. As punishment, the king had Bianhe's left foot severed. Bianhe

presented the stone again to the next king and suffered a similar fate with his right foot. When the third king came to the throne, Bianhe held onto his jade stone and cried his heart out at the foot of Jingshan. To the messenger who was sent to inquire about his grief, he said, "I'm not sad over the loss of my feet. But I am sad over the fact that a precious jade is regarded as a common stone and an honest man be taken as a liar." Whereupon this king ordered that the stone be cut open, and a precious jade was revealed. That jade was named after Bianhe in his honor.

39. "Zhounan," "Zhaonan," "Zhengfeng," and "Weifeng" are ballads from feudal states recorded under "Ballads" in *Book of Poetry*. See note 50 in "The Poet and Her Chronicler."
40. The records are found in: (1) James Legge (tr.), *Analects*, in *The Chinese Classics*, Vol. I, Book XIII "Tsze Lu," Chapter 18, p. 270; and (2) James Legge (tr.), *Mencius*, in *The Chinese Classics*, Vol. II, Part II "Li Lau," Chapter 33, p. 340. Both were published by Hong Kong University Press, 1960. Since *Analects* and *Mencius* are two of the *Four Books* of Confucian canon, it is easy to be confused over the quotations from them. "In the first story He Shuangqing's uncle treated a story by Mencius (372–289 B.C.) as something Confucius (552–479 B.C.) edited, when Confucius predated Mencius. In the second story a sheep, not a chiekcn, was the animal involved. Neither was He Shuangqing aware of these mistakes when she retold the stories."
41. *Doctrine of the Mean* (*Zhongyong*) was originally part of the *Book of Rites. Doctrine of the Mean* was authored by Confucius' grandson, Zisi 子思, to enlarge upon certain general principles of Confucius in relation to the nature of man and the right conduct of people on earth. It was combined with three other works to make up the four basic Confucian classics by the Neo-Confucian, Zhu Xi 朱熹 (1130–1200) of the Song dynasty. The three other works are *Analects* (論語), *The Great Learning* (大學), and the *Mencius* (孟子). For the *Book of Rites* or *Li ji*, see note 15 above.
42. Li Yunchou 李雲綢 was an honest and direct, yet patient man, who had the capacity for work. He was also a filial son. Corruption in officialdom where he served discouraged him, after which he

applied himself to his studies. Duan Yuhan and Shen Zhilin helped and encouraged him in his studies and writing. See *Xiqing sanji*, p. 139.

43. Cangjie 倉頡 was thought to have been an official of the Yellow Emperor (Huangdi 黃帝, 3rd millennium B.C.). He is attributed with the invention of Chinese writing through observing the tracings made by the animals and birds on the sand.
44. Both attitudes—compassion toward all animate life and absention from meat and wine—have their origin in Buddhism.
45. Zheng Chi'an 鄭癡菴 did ten or more scrolls of Mount Qixia, which is located in the northeast of Nanjing. He then invited his best friend, Chao Nazhai 巢納齋, to "explore" Mount Qixia through his paintings with him, while they drank together. The paintings depicted the two friends roaming through Mount Qixia. They had with them a servant boy who at various times, was either serving them wine or grinding ink for them to write poetry (written on many rocks in the scrolls). They also played the *qin* zither amidst the splendor of the mountain views. See *Xiqing sanji*, p. 158.
46. Bi Keshan 畢柯山 was a scholar friend of Shi Zhenlin's. A noble-minded individual, Keshan was generous and had little patience with inhumanity. Being a kindly eccentric, he attracted and was attracted by people with similar traits. See *Xiqing sanji*, pp. 97, 163–64, 167–69 and 171.
47. Mount Tai (泰山) was one of the sacred mountains in China located in the center of Shandong 山東 province.
48. The mermaids of the South Seas are believed to live and spin under water. Their tears are believed to turn into pearls.
49. The old Chinese custom of sending a branch of a tree to remind a traveler of the passing of time and of the sender's wish for the latter's early return. The idea is communication.
50. Nüwa, see note 12 above.
51. It was believed that the Dragon King resided in a crystal palace at the bottom of the sea and that he possessed fabulous treasures in his palace.
52. An intercalary month (閏月 *runyue*) is an extra month in the lunar

calendar inserted seven times in nineteen years to make up the deficiency of the lunar year to the solar year.

53. *Xiucai* 秀才 was a first degree graduate who had passed the local examination in the old Chinese civil service system and who was now qualified for the provincial examination.
54. Calling back the soul *zhao hun* (招魂) was once an ancient ritual done for the dead to prevent the soul from wandering without a home. It has been later applied to an afflicted individual whose spirit is feared to be leaving his body on account of his condition. The idea is to render some comfort and assurance to an afflicted person or creature, as in He Shuangqing's line of "To help the butterfly call back her soul."
55. Bamboo slips on which oracular verses are written as responses from the gods when consulted by the faithful.
56. "Zheng 鄭 and Wei 衛 ": same as "Zhengfeng" and "Weifeng." See note 39 above.
57. Zhao Fengqi 趙鳳岐 was a scholar and poet. He was a friend of Shi Zhenlin's and was unconventional, yet strict in his Confucian view. A story was told by Shi (see *Xiqing sanji*, p. 32) of Zhao Fengqi and his family succumbing to malaria in an epidemic in 1730 in Nanhuang 南隍, when those who believed in Shamanism urged him to join them in their prayers and sacrifice. Instead, Fengqi wrote a poem dedicated to the Sovereign on High in the heavens. This he gave to the Shaman believers and told them, "What you sing, the gods can't enjoy. Why don't you chant my poem?" They did and everyone recovered.

The Poetry

咏蛙

蓮葉層開水面樓暗香半落
便生愁仙郎為解無情網夜
雨春思說到秋　映水鄉閒坐
綠殘蒹葦茶苦敢嫌饑何方
可化銀蟾去但願身輕不願肥

The Frog

Lotus leaves by layers were parted,
Exposing the water to the pavilion.
Hidden fragrance wafted to delight,
Then sired grief in its wake.
The immortal having untied
The ruthless net,
Showers me nightly with gentle rain
From spring to fall.

Reflected by the water, leisurely
I now sit on the grass jetty.
The smartweed is bitter—
I dare not complain of hunger.
Any way to transform myself
Into the toad on the moon?
I only wish to become weightless,
Not to get fat.

淡寫

淡寫涼紅叩玉皇碧雲
吹下斷腸霜嫩愁細印
黃金粟一夜花神又
費忙

Lightly Sketched

Lightly I sketch the chilled blooms,
Pray to the supreme diety.
The blue clouds have blown in
Some heart-breaking frost.
Signs of tender sadness
Are imprinted on the golden millet—
Throughout the night the goddess of flowers
Must have been busy gathering the fallen petals.

更漏

更漏秋衣就晚晴好山能照病
容清離魂附草為螢火幽恨
如冰化水晶燕後新鴻連復斷
雨邊殘月死還生小窗夜色從
來淡便為燈花坐到明

Resunning Garments

To air again the autumn garments
I use the evening sun.
The beautiful mountain can ease somewhat
My sickly countenance.
If only my spirit could leave my body
To become a firefly among the weeds,
My inner grievance would emerge like ice
And turn into pure crystal!

After the swallows the wild geese
Fly in and out of formation;
By the rainpool the shattered moon
Is coming back to life.
Through the small window the glow
Of the night sky is usually dim,
I'll use it as a lamp,
Sit up till dawn.

和白羅九首 其一

未許焚修閑小菴冰
心無數似澄潭流
遽桂怪儀時燕淵
薄謹情病後發

Nine Poems Harmonizing Bailuo

I.

Since I can't fulfill my vow
Of retiring to a nunnery,
My frozen heart is impassive
Like a still pool.
Don't blame the hungry swallow
For being late at building his nest;
When the cocoon silk is thin,
Who pities the sick silkworm?

其二

今年青雨斷秋雲
為補新租又典裙
留得護郎輕絮暖
妾心始覺敢嫌君

II.

This year's ample rain
Cuts off the autumn clouds.
As usual I pawn my skirt
To make up for the next rent.
Since I can preserve the padded jacket
To keep my husband warm,
My heart is like honey,
I don't reject him.

其三

細綴麻鞋線幾重
採樵明日上西峰作
寒夜風偏急莫向
郎吹盡向儂

III.

Stitching closely to make a pair of hemp boots
Calls for many layers of thread.
To pick kindling tomorrow
I'll go up the west peak.
The sudden chill in the night
Is accompanied by a fierce wind—
Don't blow at my husband,
Concentrate on me.

其四

冷廚烟濕障低房
鬢畫棲桐謝鳳凰
野菜自挑寒自洗
菊花雖痛奈何霜

IV.

Smoky and damp, the cold kitchen
Is on the lower level.
Using *wutong* wood for fuel
Calls for an apology to the phoenix.
I pick weeds for greens,
In the cold I wash them;
The chrysanthemum may suffer,
What can you do about the frost?

其五

命如蟬翼愧輕綃
舊与鄰娥一樣嬌
阿母見兒還認否
苦黄生面春红消

V.

My life is fragile
Like a cicada's wing.
I used to be as beautiful
As the neighbor's daughter—
When Mother sees me,
Will she recognize her child
Now that bitter yellow has robbed
My face of its cheerful pink?

其六

漫遊春酸一點心痛
中瑙夢易消沉鏡
錄已責酬方藥自
制楊枝照水簪

VI.

Deluged by spring's tempering
Is my little heart;
In illness dreams are infrequent—
They fade easily.
Having pawned my mirror,
Gold hairpins to buy medicine,
I must whittle some willow branches
To pin up my hair by the reflection of the water.

其七

四屏山影遠如臺
郎買寒薪下幾回
歸後勸郎晨晏起
日高私禁外人催

VII.

The shadow of Siping Mountain is cast
Far out like a plateau.
My husband has been hauling wood
Up and down in the cold.
When he returns, I shall plead
With him to sleep late;
Even when the sun is up,
I will not let anyone disturb him.

其八

家雞双宿笑棲鸞比
翼齊肩再業冠燈
晴結花光變綠窗
稜堪倚勝闌干

VIII.

The family chickens are happily paired:
They go about wing to wing,
Shoulder to shoulder, comb to comb.
Yet when the lamp dims, its wick turns to a bud,
Its flame takes on a greenish hue,
I choose to lean on the stove
Rather than on the railing
[Where the chickens can be seen].

其九

妾住衡门傍綵楼夜
香吹下隔簾懸袖
闲庭盡秋红白裹
草殘陽分遠遊

IX.

I live next to a painted house
Behind a humble door.
When the scent of the tuberose wafts over,
I'm sad behind the screen.
I have depleted my feelings
For the autumn's glow;
Fading grass, setting sun
Make me dream of going far away.

步寧溪韻 其一

月魂滴艷綃山倒細
切霞膏嚥冰臆紅
粉蒸為窈窕雲青
天盡變芙蓉色

After Ningxi's Rhyme

I.

Moonlight trickles its brilliance
Onto the slope of Xiaoshan,
Splinters the sunset's glow
Into choked ice, it seems.
The pink mist ascending,
Becomes elegant clouds;
It turns the whole sky
Into lotus hues.

其二

家住華陽第八天巷
西流水巷南田手攜
秀線嫩如雨欲繫
鴛鴦何可憐

II.

My abode is in Huayang's
Eighth heaven,
On the west a brook,
On the south a field.
I finger the fine silk
Tender as rain—
I long to use it
In match-making for the true lovers.

其三

妾容憔悴郎顏老
小庭土白塵難掃
粧丹貧賤不成花
卻將富貴輸芳草

III.

My face is haggard,
My husband's creased.
The dust in the little court is chalky,
Difficult to sweep away.
The peony impoverished
Yields no bloom;
Instead, it relinquishes
Its nutrients to the herbs.

其四

曾記桑陰學種瓜
與郎消渴餉新
茶夜涼帶雨開窗
坐放月吹燈睛績麻

IV.

I recall how in the mulberry shade
I learned to plant melons,
Quenched my husband's thirst
By offering him tea.
In the cool night while sick,
I'd sit at the open window,
Let in the moonlight by blowing out the lamp
To weave hemp in the dark.

其五

書生漫買情才癖
妾在田家靜安怡
雨後黃鸝作一聲
春愁喚上青青葉

V.

The scholars came to appreciate talent
But received little response from me;
Now I'm peacefully
Settled in a farm family.
After the rain
The oriole's sudden cry
Summons my spring sorrow
Into the green, green arbor.

其六

雲意陰晴向晚猜
林前無地可徘徊
縱教化作孤飛鳳
不到秦家弄玉臺

VI.

Impending snow, cloudy or sunny,
Becomes the evening's riddle;
In front of my bed
There's no space for pacing.
Even if I could become
A lonely phoenix,
I'd not fly
To the Jade Pavilion of Qin.

其七

斜羅不帶零星片月
綻金衣黃對綠白煙
遙夢抱梅花繁霜
夜洗佳人面

VII.

The constellation is askew,
Only remnants remain.
Mending a winter jacket
Entails much sewing.
Dreamily the white mist
Embraces the plum blossoms;
Thick frost bathes
My face in the night air.

和夢覲

風吹細雨濕柴扉十
斂後田事業微歲旱
木棉花未發杼寒梭
冷停空機

Harmonizing Mengzhan

The wind sweeps fine rain,
Wetting the rustic gate.
There's little to do
In the ten *mu* of paddy field.
The weather's been dry;
The cotton's yet to bloom;
The shuttles are cold;
I lean on the empty loom.

茶菴

寒雲欲去吹還倒隱
送殘暉印孤騰下
和雙淚度荊山百
花暗帶消魂色

The Plantain

The more the scattered clouds try to right themselves,
The more they are blown askew;
Through their clefts they let in the last rays
To express my feelings.
Bianhe shed tears
Over Jingshan to mourn
Flowers with their hidden beauty
Not perceived by the common man.

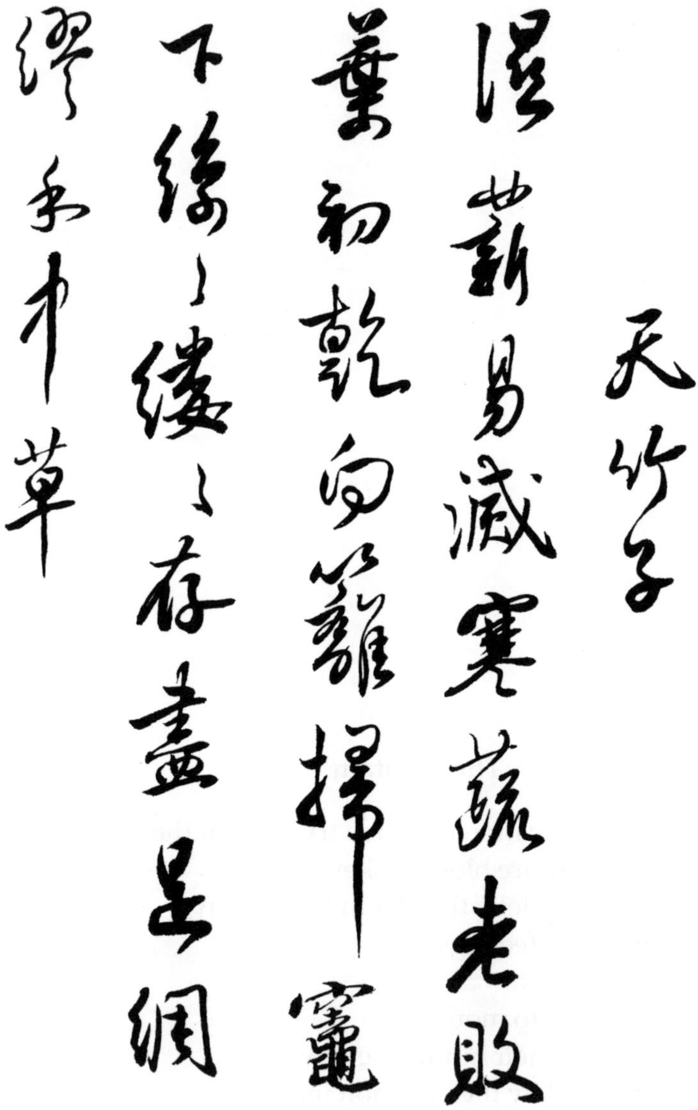

The Heavenly Bamboo

Wet firewood smothers easily;
Winter vegetables are old.
Matted leaves, finally dry,
Are swept to the bamboo fence;
Under the stove are stored
Strands and strands of grass
In tight bundles
Hand-bound for fuel.

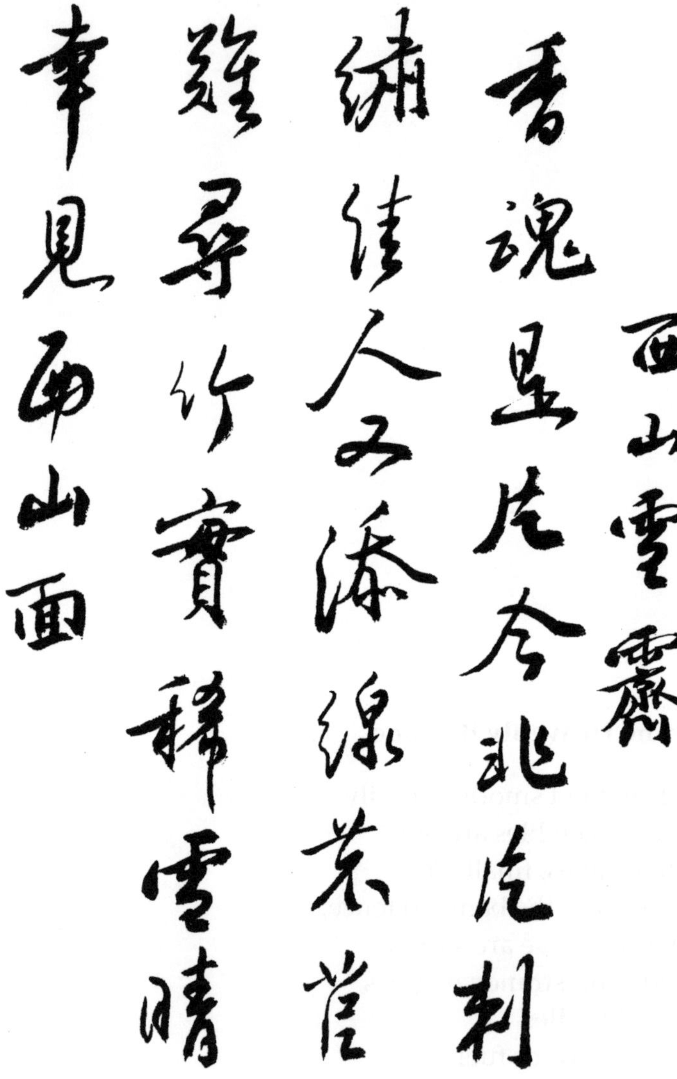

Snow Clearing over the Western Mountains

The clouds in shavings
Have now vanished.
The lady adds another thread
To her embroidery.
Plantain is difficult to find,
Bamboo shoots are scarce;
Snow lifts, happily unveiling
The face of the western mountains.

柳絮

柳絮多情已化萍
素魂紅怨淡無聲
似聞燕子三更語
月過花梢又不明

Willow Catkins

The willow catkins with sentiment
Have become like duckweeds;
Their pure spirit, drifts quietly
In the current of fallen petals.
Listen! Are those swallows
Chattering at third watch?
Sailing over the top of the flowering tree,
The moon darkens again.

秋荷十首 其一

錦鱗無信泣秋風心
似芭蕉卷未鬆幽性
耐霜霜不忍梅花探淡
菊花濃

Ten Poems on the Autumn Lotus

I.

I receive no communications,
Even the crickets cry for me;
My heart is like the rolled plantain leaf
Still to loosen.
The chrysanthemum can stand frost,
Though the frost tries to be kind.
It is at its peak of bloom,
While the plum has yet to come into its own.

其二

蘄意梅魂兩自知
少陽人去鸞回時仙
郎肯荼蘼神居顛
酬人間怨女祠

II.

The chrysanthemum and the plum
Both know their own time.
At sunset the farmhands leave,
The egrets return.
Does the immortal care to sacrifice
To the goddess of flowers?
Let him also offer
At the shrine of grievous women.

其三

女郎清態曉涼吹
露滴盈兒冷眼窺
蓮子有心秋正苦
不憐明月更憐誰

III.

The lady's grievance is cooled
By the morning breeze;
Dew drops on lotus leaves,
While little fish watch quietly.
The lotus seed harbors a heart
That turns bitter in autumn;
Where but the moon
Can you place your tenderness?

其四

月明如水蝶金無微
鑪初消凜凜孤夜雨
又來紅欲碎殺人
相見淚應枯

IV.

Moonlight is as cold as water,
All the butterflies have vanished.
The moon's feeble light weakens;
The land becomes cold, desolate.
Night rain resumes,
Shattering the petals;
The mermaids, on meeting,
Will be drained of tears.

其五

淚盡鮫珠不顧開
前生香孽此生猜
一枝遠寄千絲斷
七月江南雁早來

V.

Tears exhausted,
The mermaids have no desire to shed pearls.
What retribution from my last life
I can only guess at in this.
I sent a branch of lotus away,
Severing its milky strands;
In the seventh month
The wild geese are returning early this year.

其六

霞邊新雁月邊人
菱荇爭欺菡萏貧
黃鳥可知情白鳥
野壤花賤不如春

VI.

The sunset silhouettes the early wild geese;
The moon, the person.
The water chestnut is aggressive,
The lotus is impoverished.
Does the yellow bird ever
Take pity on the white bird?
Now, unlike spring,
Flowers in the wild pond are unprized.

其七

淡影為春鏡裏看
水心擬夜難安葉
遮猶雨花遮露香
護鴛鴦夢可容

VII.

The autumn lotus demurely views
Its thin reflection in the pond.
The current's sway
Allows it little peace at night.
Its leaves screen off the blustering rain;
Its flowers, the frost;
Tenderly it protects the mandarin ducks
Even when their dreams may be chilled.

其八

癡聾無夢攬芳年懸
在銀蟾桂子先補遍
西湖花五色傷心可
是女媧天

VIII.

The love-sick mandarin drake is dreamless,
Enjoying his prime.
My weary feeling began
Before the autumn moon and cassia bloom.
Having to mend the many colored flowers
Around West Lake,
Will this grieve
The heart of Nüwa?

其九

五色天邊寂寞宵
淚研秋粉月中描
細收花片輕輕碾
搓就香丸帳裡燒

IX.

The colorful horizon
Ushers in a lonely dusk.
I use my tears to grind autumn pollen
For sketching in the moonlight.
Carefully I pick up
Every lotus petal and lightly grind,
Then shape it into pellets
To scent my curtained bed.

其十

香丸燒盡碧煙多
萍水姻緣薄宦訛
從此蓬頭分不得
裂紅裁翠補漁蓑

X.

The scented pellets are burnt,
Giving off blue smoke.
The chanced union of two people—
A fate how deceiving!
From now on since I can't
Be separated from you,
I'll cut up remnants
To mend your coir cloak.

浣溪沙

暖雨無情漏幾絲牧童斜
插嫩花枝小田新麥上場時
汲水種瓜偏怒早忍烟炊
黍又嗔遲日長酸透軟腰
肢

To the Tune of *Huan xi sha*

Warm rain without sentiment, a few dripping strands,
The cowherd holding a branch of flowers at a slant,
It's time for the new wheat
To appear in the small field.
Drawing water from the well to plant melons, I was
Spitefully rebuked for being too early;
Withstanding the smoke in cooking,
I was scolded for taking too much time.
The day is long and pain
Goes through my tender frame.

望江南

春不見尋過野橋西染夢淡紅欺
粉蝶鎖愁濃綠騷黃鸝幽恨
莫重提人不見相見是還非拜月
有香空惹袖惜花無淚可沾衣
山遠夕陽低

To the Tune of *Wang Jiangnan*

Spring, you are nowhere,
I look for you over the rustic bridge in the west.
You're a vision dyed light pink
To trick the butterflies;
You lock your sadness in dark green
To mislead the golden oriole.
My deep sorrow,
Don't bring it up again.

That person, he's nowhere;
Our meeting will be only futile.
When I worship the moon goddess,
Incense stirs my sleeves;
When I mourn the fading of the flowers,
I have no more tears to stain my dress.
The mountain, far away;
The sun, low.

濕羅衣

世間難吐只幽情淚珠嚥盡
還生手撚殘花無言倚屏
鏡裏相看自驚瘦亭亭春
容不是秋容不是可是雙卿

To the Tune of *Shi luoyi*

There's nothing more difficult
To express than hidden sorrow;
Though tears are completely swallowed,
They'll well up again.
I finger the dying flowers;
Speechless, I lean on the screen.
I'm alarmed at my image in the mirror—
I'm sedate and thin,
But my face is not that of spring,
Nor of autumn,
Is it really Shuangqing!

玉京秋　自題種花小影

眉半斂春紅已全褪舊愁還欠畫中
塵影萬人雖閃新病三分未醒淡胭
脂空費輕染涼生夜月華如洗素娥無
玷翠袖啼痕堪黯海棠邊曾沾萬點
悵追來尋常梳裹酸鹹都厭粉汗
凝香蘸碧水羅帕時揩冰簟有誰念原
是花神輕貶

To the Tune of *Yujing qiu*
(Colophon for the Painting "Planting Melons")

Brow knitted,
My youthful bloom has faded—
Much old sorrow I still owe.
My thin image in the painting,
Inescapable and mortifying!
I'm still drowsy from my new illness—
Even pink rouge
Is a waste of effort.
The cold intensifies during the night;
The bright moon, as if refreshed by a rain,
Is pure, flawless.
On my blue-green sleeves are tear stains;
By their flowery edge
Are countless spots.
No wonder lately
When I comb my hair, bind my feet,
Life, whether salty or sour, is weary for me.
Sweat under my powder brings out the perfume.
I dip my handkerchief into the blue water
To wipe again the bamboo mat.
Who is concerned about me,
A goddess of flowers
Exiled temporarily on earth?

二郎神　菊花

絲絲脆柳裊破淡煙依舊向落日秋山
影裡還喜花枝未瘦苦雨重陽挨過
了虧耐到小春時候知今夜蘸微霜蝶
去自垂首　生受新寒浸骨病來還又
可是我雙卿薄倖撇你黃昏靜後月冷
闌干人不寐鎮幾夜未鬆金扣枉辜卻開
向貧家愁處欲澆無酒

To the Tune of *Erlang shen* (The Chrysanthemum)

The frail willow, like silk,
Gracefully breaks up the light mist as usual
Into shadows on the autumn hill at sunset.
I'm glad your flowering branches
Have not withered.
You've endured bitter rain through Chongyang,
Now made the tenth month.
I know tonight
There'll be a touch of frost;
By the time butterflies leave,
You'll naturally lower your head.

Intensely
You are suffering in your bones
Pain from the season's first chill.
Unfortunately I'll have to be ungracious,
To desert you when evening's quiet comes.
With the moon so cold over the railing,
I cannot sleep;
For many nights I've stayed up
Without letting down the bed curtains.
In vain you bloom for a poor family;
There's no wine for you to dispel your sorrow.

寄孫鸞

乍寒信染早霜意初來碧彩添襯宿
鬢擁梳亂裹帕羅齊鬢著情牛素裙來浣
摺痕邊斷綠雙損玉腕近看如瀾可香腮
還嫩　算一生憑捷也拚鬼便化粉成灰
嫁時先忖錦恩花情散被蘿煙薰盡
東篇卻嫌綯緩冷潮回熱潮誰問歸
去將棉曬取又晚炊相近

To the Tune of *Ji gu luan*

As luck would have it, the midday freeze
Began when my intermittent fever was coming on.
I put on an extra blue jacket;
My chignon being dishevelled from sleep,
Carelessly I tied a scarf to keep my hair in place.
In my haste I neglected to wash my plain skirt;
On its folding seam
Are a couple of silk threads broken.
A close look at my wrists shows they're calloused;
Still, my cheeks are youthful.

At least I've survived all the miseries in life,
Even though I may be reduced to ashes.
At the time of marriage
I had dreams of happiness—
Guess they've turned to smoke in the kitchen.
At the eastern fallow field there were rebukes for lunch
was late;
Tides of chill overcome me—
My fever, who is concerned?
Must dash home to retrieve the cotton being sunned;
Very soon dinner needs to be tended to again.

惜黃花慢　孤雁

碧盡遙天但暮霞散綺碎剪紅鮮聽時愁
近望時怕遠孤鴻一個去向誰邊素霜已冷蘆
花渚更休倩鷗鷺相憐暗自眠鳳凰縱好寧
是姻緣淒涼勸你無言趁一沙半水且度流
年稻粱初盡網羅正苦夢魂易驚幾家
寒烟斷腸可似嬋娟意寸心裡多少纏綿
夜來閒倦飛誤宿平田

To the Tune of *Xi huanghua man* (Lonely Wild Goose)

Azure over the distant sky
Except for scattered,
Red fragments of the sunset.
When I listen, I dread seeing you close by;
When I look, I fear you are far away.
Lonely wild goose,
To whose side are you heading?
The white frost is already caking the rush bank;
Don't dally,
Or be envious of the loving seagulls—
Go to sleep quietly by yourself.
To be of a phoenix pair is splendid;
After all, their marriage is made in heaven.

With grief I implore you not to complain;
Make use of the sandbar, little pond,
Pass your fleeting days for the time being.
Your chance at the grain is gone,
Nets are stretched everywhere to get you;
Even in dreams your spirit will be disturbed.
Cold smoke rises from only a few houses.
Your grief for your mate
In your little heart
Must be inextricable!
The night is not yet over;
Tired, you may lose your chance of alighting
Except in an open field.

鳳凰臺上憶吹簫　殘燈

已情忘吹欲明誰影向儂無簇如螢聽去
階寒雨滴破破更將自懨了耿耿難斷處也
忘多情香膏盡芳心未冷且伴雙卿
星星漸微不動還望你淹煎有個花生
勝野塘風亂搖曳漁燈辛苦秋蛾散
後人已病病減何曾相看久朦朧成睡睡
去空驚

To the Tune of *Fenghuang tai shang yi chuixiao* (The Dying Lamp Wick)

Already dim but left unblown,
You want to brighten but who'll pull you up?
You face me like a firefly without a flame.
Listen to the cold rain on the tamped-earth steps—
It'll drip through the third watch.
Alone, placid, yet disquiet,
You're undecided,
Because you are too emotional.
Your oil is exhausted,
But your heart is still warm.
Stay awhile to keep me company.

You're now a spark,
You're getting smaller, languishing.
I hope while you linger,
You will flare.
It's better than being the fisherman's lamp,
Wavering in the wind on the open sea,
Toiling in the trail of autumn moths.
I'm already sick,
Will not improve.
After gazing at you for a while,
I may doze off
To sleep away my empty fears.

薄倖　詠瘦

依々孤影渾似夢憑誰喚醒受多少蝶嗔
蜂與有藥難醫花證最怕時那得工夫淒
涼自整紅爐等　總訴盡濃愁滴乾清
淚寬懸娥眉不看去過西來先午便放卻
更深宵永正千迴萬轉欲眠仍起斷鴻叫破
殘陽冷晚山如鏡小叢籠煙鎖佳人翠袖懨々
為春歸望早　只恐東風來肯

To the Tune of *Boxing* (Ode to Malaria)

Abiding with me is my lonely shadow;
I'm confused as in a dream—
Who'll wake me?
I endure much scolding from the butterfly,
Ire from the bee;
No wonder that even with medicine
I don't improve.
During the harvest season
Is there a moment for rest?
Mournfully I rekindle the brazier
To brew my medicine.

On the whole I've unfolded my sorrows,
Exhausted my tears.
No one knows the killing oppression I suffer—
Getting through the evening,
Facing the midday,
The day drags and night is forever.
Just after much turning
When I'm about to fall asleep,
It's time to rise again.

The sad honking of the wild geese
Breaks the sunset's afterglow,
Chilling it.
The evening hill is like a mirror;
The small rustic gate
In the shrouding mist confines me.
I believe my shortness of breath will soon cease.
How I wish spring will return early;
My only fear—the east wind may not agree.

一剪梅

寒熱如潮勢未平病起無言自掃
前庭瓊花魂斷碧天愁推下淒涼
一個雙卿 夜冷荒雞懶不鳴擬雪
猜霜怕雨貪晴最閑時候妾偏忙
纔喜雙卿又怨雙卿

To the Tune of *Yijian mei*

Chills, fevers come like tides—
My condition is not stable.
Speechless after a bout,
Alone I sweep the front court.
Tangerine flowers have faded,
Sky a mournful blue.
I push away my sorrows,
I'm alone.

When the evening is chilly,
Even the wild cock becomes lazy about crowing.
Will it snow, will it frost?
I fear rain, I hope for sunshine.
When things are quiet,
That's when I'm busy.
One instant, I'm happy;
Another, I'm scolded.

摸魚兒

春初晴晚霞西現寒山烟外青淺紫紅乾雲
容香覆尖印叢泥縱數人語亂忙去倚柴扉
空留滴滴顆相思一線向新月搓圓穿愁貫
恨珠淚總成串　黃昏後殘熱誰憐細喘
小窗風射如箭春紅秋白無情豔一朵似儂難
選重見遠聽說道傷心已受殷勤餞斜陽
利眼休更望天涯天涯只是幾片冷雲展

To the Tune of *Mo yuer*

Glad the rain has stopped,
Sunset aglow in the west;
Cold mountains beyond the mist in gradations of blue
and green.
Where it's dry on the moss I can tread,
Leaving traces on the mud still soft and purple.
Too much noise here;
I'd better go lean on the rustic gate.
I haven't fulfilled my deep wish—
Our love is of one thread,
I'll twist it into a thread under the new moon,
Use it to string all my sorrows and regrets
In the way my pearly tears do fall.

After twilight
I'm still feverish—who'll pity my panting?
Through the small window the wind shoots like arrows.
Blooming spring, elegant autumn, both beautiful, but
without emotion.
Rare is the flower like myself.
Our meeting will be distant;
I've heard that the broken heart
Has already accepted the farewell feast.
The low sun hurts my eyes,
I mustn't gaze at the horizon anymore—
After all, there are only
A few cold clouds expanding on the horizon.

鳳凰台上憶吹簫

寸々微雲絲々殘照有無明滅難消正
斷魂々斷閃々搖々望々山々水々人去々隱々
迢々從今後酸々楚々只似今宵青遙
問天不應看小々雙卿嫋々無聊更見誰
誰見誰痛花嬌誰望歡々喜々偷素粉
寫々描々誰還管生々世々夜々朝々

To the Tune of *Fenghuang tai shang yi chuixiao*

Tiny, tiny snippets of clouds,
Silky, silky strands of sunset's afterglow.
They are, they are not; they glow, they will not cease.
Just when they affect my spirit, my spirit gives way.
How they glitter and sway!
Look, look! Hill after hill, water after water!
When a person dies,
His spirit hovers, hovers among the rushes far, far away.
From now on
My life will be sour, sour, bitter, bitter—
Just like tonight.

Oh, blue yonder,
I've asked Heaven but received no reply.
Look at little, little Shuangqing,
Weak, weak, ennui.
Who do I see, who sees me?
Who feels tenderly for beautiful flowers?
Who looks forward happily, happily,
Secretly using pollen
To write, write, sketch, sketch?
Who would care life after life, generation after generation,
Dusk after dusk, dawn after dawn?

春從天上來 梅花

自笑懨懨費半晌春忙去看花尖玉容
憔悴知爲誰添病來分與花嬌正臘衣
誰洗春波冷素腕愁沾硬東風極寒
香一度新月纖纖 多情備天墜粉偏只
累雙卿夢裡空招與蝶招魂猜驚拭淚
夜深偷誦楞嚴有傷春佳句酸和苦生
死俱甜祝花年向觀音稽首摯偏靈籤

To the Tune of *Chun cong tianshang lai* (Plum Blossoms)

Placidly I laugh at myself,
Taking time from the busy season of spring
To examine the tips of your petals.
You look languid—
I wonder for whom you multiply.
Since my illness,
I share the regret with flowers.
The winter clothes demand washing—
Spring water is cold,
Immersing my wrists I dread.
The east wind is harsh;
In vain have you been fragrant during winter.
The new moon is slim.

Kind Heaven pollinates you.
This only beguiles me
To seek my fortune in my dreams,
To help the butterfly call back her soul,
To wipe away the tears for the oriole.
In the middle of the night
Stealthily I read the *Lengyen jing*.
In it I found a beautiful line regretting spring:
"Whether sad or bitter,
Life, death are both sweet."
I pray a happy year for you;
I bow my head to the Goddess of Mercy,
I've consulted every bamboo slip in the lot.

春從天上來

餉耕

紫陌春晴懮顏裏春紗自餉春耕小梅春
瘦細草春明春田步步春生記那年春好
向春燕說破春情到於今想春箋春淚
都化春冰　憐春痛春春幾被一層春烟
鎖住春鶯贈與春儂遞將春你是儂
是你春靈算春頭春尾也難算春夢
春醒甚春魔做一春春病為春誤雙卿

To the Tune of *Chun cong tianshang lai* (Bringing Lunch to the Field)

The purple path is alive with spring,
I cover my forehead with a light spring scarf,
Set out to bring lunch to the spring planting.
The small plum is spring-thin in blossoms;
The fine grass is spring-radiant;
Every step in the spring field is resplendent with spring
growth.
I recall the year when spring was beautiful,
I told my spring emotions to the spring swallow.
As for now,
When I think of spring poems, spring tears,
They have all become spring ice to me.

How many springs have I felt tenderly toward spring,
loved spring?
A layer of spring mist
Cages the spring oriole—
Let me make a gift of it to you, Spring;
I'll hand it to you, Spring.
This is me, the same as your spring spirit.
I can count your spring beginnings and spring endings,
But I can't count all the spring dreams, spring awakenings
you've evoked.
What spring demon brings
This spring illness for the spring?
Spring, you've deceived me!

Selected Bibliography

I. General

Campbell, Joseph, ed. *The Portable Jung*. Translated by R.F.C. Hull. New York: The Viking Press Inc., 1971.

Chan, Wingtsit. *Neo-Confucianism, etc.: Essays (English and Chinese)*. Compiled by Charles K. H. Chen. Hanover, New Hampshire: Oriental Society, 1969.

Chang Chung-yuan, trans. *Original Teachings of Ch'an Buddhism, Selected from the Transmission of the Lamp*. New York: Random House, Pantheon Books, 1969.

Chen Menglei 陳夢雷 (orig. comp.) and Jiang Tingxi 蔣廷錫 et al., comps. *Gujin tushu jicheng* 古今圖書集成 (至1725) [Encyclopedia of Chinese Works from Early Times to the Present (1725)], Vols. 41–45. Reprint of 1728 edition. Shanghai: Zhonghua shuju 中華書局 , 1934.

Chu Yuan. *Li Sao (An Elegy on Encountering Sorrows) in English and Chinese*. Translated by Lim Boon Keng. Shanghai: Shangwu yinshuguan 商務印書館 , 1935.

Cihai 辭海 . Shanghai: Zhonghua shuju 中華書局 , 1936.

Cranmer-Byng, L. and S. A. Kapadiat, eds. *Musing of a Chinese Mystic, Selections from the Philosophy of Chuangtze*. Wisdom of the East Series. Reprint. London: John Murray, 1927.

Creel, Harlee G. *Chinese Thoughts from Confucius to Mao Tsetung*. Attitudes of Destiny Series. Chicago: University of Chicago Press, 1953.

A Dictionary of Buddhism, Chinese-Sanskrit-English-Thai. Reprint. Taipei: Tianhua chuban gongsi 天華出版公司 , 1982.

A Dictionary of Chinese Buddhist Terms with Sanskrit and English Equivalents and a Sanskrit-Pali Index. London: Kegan Paul, Trench, Trubner and Company Ltd., 1934.

Fairbank, John K. and Edwin O. Reischauer. *China: Tradition and Transformation*. New York: Houghton Mifflin Company, 1973.

Feng Yu-lan. *A History of Chinese Philosophy*, 2 vols. Translated by Derk Bodde. Princeton: Princeton University Press, 1953.

Goddard, Dwight, ed. *A Buddhist Bible*. Boston: Beacon Press, 1970.

Goodrich, L. Carrington. *A Short History of the Chinese Peoples*. New York: Harper and Brothers, 1943.

Hawkes, David, trans. and comp. *Chu Tzu (The Songs of the South), an Ancient Chinese Anthology of Poems by Chu Yuan and Other Poets*. Harmondsworth, Middlesex: Penguin Books, 1985.

He Shuangqing 賀雙卿 . *Xueya Xuan ji* 雪壓軒集 [Collection from the Snow Crushed Studio]. Edited by Zhang Shoulin 張壽林 . Beijing: Wenhua xueshe faxing 文化學社發行 , 1927.

Hsu Kai-yu, trans. and ed. Preface to *Twentieth Century Chinese Poetry: An Anthology*. Ithaca: Cornell University Press, 1970.

Huang Dashou 黃大受 . *Zhongguo jindai shi* 中國近代史 [Chinese Contemporary History], Vol. 1. Shanghai: Zhongguo tushu gongsi 中國圖書公司 , 1959.

Japanese-English Buddhist Dictionary. Tokyo: Daito Suppansha, 1979.

Legge, James, trans. *The Analects*. The Chinese Classics, Vol. I. Hong Kong: Hong Kong University Press, 1960.

———. *Mencius*. The Chinese Classics, Vol. II. Hong Kong: Hong Kong University Press, 1960.

Lin Yutang, trans. and ed. *The Wisdom of Laotse*. The Modern Library. New York: Random House, 1948.

———. *Lin Yutang's Chinese-English Dictionary of Modern Usage*. Hong Kong: The Chinese University of Hong Kong, 1972.

Liu Daren 劉達人 . *Liu's Chinese-English Dictionary* 劉氏漢英辭典 . New York: The Asian Associate, 1978.

Liu, James J. Y. *The Art of Chinese Poetry*. Chicago: University of Chicago Press, 1962.

Mathew, R. H. *Mathew's Chinese-English Dictionary*. Cambridge, Mass.: Harvard University Press, 1947.

May, Rollo. *The Courage to Create*. New York: Bantam Books, Inc., 1975.

Needham, Joseph. *History of Sciences and Scientific Thought. Science and Civilization in China*, Vol. II. Cambridge: Cambridge University Press, 1956.

Rhys, Ernest, ed. *The Travels of Marco Polo*. Reprint. London: J. K. Dent and Sons Ltd., 1921.

Shi Zhenlin 史震林. *Xiqing sanji* 西青散記 [West Green Random Notes]. *Zhongguo wenxue zhenben congshu* 中國文學珍本叢書 [Collections of Rare Manuscripts from Chinese Literature], first collection, no. 5. Shanghai: Shanghai zazhi gongsi 上海雜誌公司, 1935.

———. *Xiqing sanji* 西青散記 [West Green Random Notes], *juan* 2. N.p.: Gujin shushi 古今書室, printed by lithographic process in early 20th century possibly.

———. *Huayang sangao* 華陽散稿 [Huayang Essays]. *Zhongguo wenxue zhenben congshu* 中國文學珍本叢書 [Collection of Rare Manuscripts from Chinese literature], first collection, no. 9. Shanghai: Shanghai zazhi gongsi 上海雜誌公司, 1935.

Sun Zuoyun 孫作雲. *Shijing yu zhoudai shehui yanjiu* 詩經與周代社會研究 [A Study of Zhou Society Through the Odes]. Beijing: Zhonghua shuju 中華書局, 1966.

Tan Zhengbi 譚正壁, ed. *Zhongguo wenxuejia dacidian* 中國文學家大辭典 [Dictionary of Chinese Writers]. Hong Kong: Wenshi chubanshe 文史出版社, 1961.

Tsui Chi 崔驥. *A Short History of Chinese Civilization* 中國文化史綱. New York: Putnam, 1943.

Van der Post, Laurens. *Jung and the Story of Our Time*. New York: Random House, Pantheon Books, 1975.

Wei Zhengtong 韋政通. *Zhongguo sixiang shi* 中國思想史 [The History of Chinese Thought]. Vol. 1. Taipei: Dalin chubanshe 大林出版社, 1979.

Werner, E.T.C. *A Dictionary of Chinese Mythology*. New York: The Julian Press, 1961.

Zhou Yifu 周億孚. *Rujia sixiang he shenghuo* 儒家思想和生活

[Confucian Thought and Life]. Hong Kong: Jingfeng yanjiushe 景風研究社, 1968.

Zhu Xi 朱熹. *Shijing pangxun* 詩經旁訓 [Lessons from the Odes]. Shanghai: Guangyi shuju 廣益書局, 1921.

II. Chinese Literature

Birch, Cyril, ed. *Anthology of Chinese Literature*, Vols. 1–2. New York: Grove Press, 1972.

Giles, Herbert A. *A History of Chinese Literature*. New York: Grove Press, 1958.

Kalgren, Bernhard. *Sound and Symbol in Chinese*. Hong Kong: Hong Kong University Press, 1933.

Lai Ming. *A History of Chinese Literature*. New York: Capricorn Books, 1964.

Li Baowei 李寶位, ed. *Zhongguo wenxue shilue* 中國文學史略 [An Outline of Chinese Literature]. Taipei: Dasheng shuju 大聖書局, 1972.

Liu Dajie 劉大杰. *Zhongguo wenxue fazhan shi* 中國文學發展史 [History of the Development of Chinese Literature], 3 vols. Shanghai: Zhonghua chubanshe 中華出版社, 1949.

Zheng Zhenduo 鄭振鐸. *Zhongguo wenxue yanjiu* 中國文學研究 [Research into Chinese Literature], 3 vols. Beijing: Zuojia chubanshe 作家出版社, 1975.

III. Poetry Anthologies

Chen Xiang 陳香, ed. *Qingdai nushiren xuanji* 清代女詩人選集 [Selections from Women Poets of the Qing Dynasty], 2 vols. Taipei: Shangwu yinshuguan 商務印書館, 1974.

Dong Chao 董潮 (Dongting 東亭), ed. "Donggao zachao 東皐雜鈔

[Random Copy]." In Wu Shenglan 吳省蘭, *Yihai Zhuchen* 藝海珠塵 [Gems from the Art World], *juan* 3. Baibu congshu jicheng 百部叢書集成. Reprint. Taipei: 1968.

Han Shiqiu 韓石秋. *Qingdai wenxue shi* 清代文學史 [History of the Literature of the Qing Dynasty]. Taiwan, Gaoxiong: Baicheng shuju 百成書局, 1973.

Li Ling 李靈. *Lidai cainu shici xuan* 歷代才女詩詞選 [Poetry Selections by Talented Women Through the Ages]. Hong Kong: Yuzhou shuju 宇宙書局, n.d.

Li Baiying 李白英. *Zhongguo lidai nuzi cixuan* 中國歷代女子詞選 [Selections of Women's Lyric Verses Through the Ages]. Shanghai: Guanghua shuju 光華書局, 1932.

Lin, Julia C. *Modern Chinese Poetry — An Introduction*. Seattle: University of Washington Press, 1973.

Nai Ding 乃鼎. *Sushou Yin* 素手吟 [The Hums of Women]. Taipei: Nanjing chuban gongsi 南京出版公司, 1979.

Tao Qiuying 陶秋英. *Zhongguo funu yu wenxue* 中國婦女與文學 [Chinese Women and Literature]. Taipei: Landeng chubanshe 藍燈出版社, 1975.

Tong Renlan 童紉蘭 and Sun Peichai 孫佩茝, eds. *Nu zuojia shici xuan* 女作家詩詞選 [Selections of Poetry by Women Writers]. Hong Kong: Lezhi chubanshe 樂知出版社, 1961.

Waley, Arthur. *Translations of 170 Chinese Poems*. London: Constable and Company, 1918.

Wang Yunzhang 王蘊章. *Ranzhi yuyun* 然脂餘韻 [Rhymes Recovered from Women Writers], 6 vols. Shanghai: Shangwu yinshuguan 商務印書館, 1918.

Wu Hao 吳灝. *Lidai mingyuan cixuan* 歷代名媛詞選 [Lyric Verses from Chinese Women Through the Ages], 6 vols. Shanghai: Mushi shanfang 木石山房, n.d.

Xu Ke 徐珂, ed. *Lidai guixiu cixuan jiping* 歷代閨秀詞選集評 [Selections and Critique of Women's Lyric Verses Through the Ages]. Shanghai: Shangwu yinshuguan 商務印書館, 1926.

Yi Baiyin 裔柏蔭 . *Lidai nu shici xuan* 歷代女詩詞選 [Selections of Women's Poetry Through the Ages]. Taipei: Dangdai tushu chubanshe 當代圖書出版社 , 1971.

Yuan Mei 袁枚 , ed. *Zhoudai shuqing shi yizhu* 周代抒情詩譯註 [Annotations on the Lyric Poetry of the Zhou Dynasty]. Shandong: Shandong renmin chubanshe 山東人民出版社 , n.d.

Zheng Zhenduo 鄭振鐸. *Chuci Tu* 楚辭圖 [Map of "The Song of the South"]. Beijing: Zhonghua shuju 中華書局 , 1963.

IV. Chinese Women

Chen Dongyuan 陳東原 . *Zhongguo funu shenghuo xi* 中國婦女生活史 [Life of Chinese Women]. Shanghai: Shangwu yinshuguan 商務印書館 , 1937.

Feng Fei 馮飛. *Nuxing lun* 女性論 [On Women]. Shanghai: Zhonghua shuju 中華書局 , 1923.

Jie Jin 解縉, et al., eds. *Gujin lienu zhuan* 古今列女傳 [Brave Women Since Ancient Times], 3 vols. N.p., printed from Ming dynasty woodblock set, 1898. In University of Michigan Asia Library collection.

Li Jiafu 李甲孚. *Zhongguo gudai de nuxing* 中國古代的女性 [Chinese Women in Ancient Times]. Taipei: Liming wenhua shiye gufen youxian gongsi 黎明文化事業股份有限公司 , 1973.

Liu Dehan 劉德漢 . *Dongzhou funu shenghuo* 東周婦女生活 [Life of Women in the Eastern Zhou Dynasty]. Taipei: Xuesheng shudian 學生書店 , 1974.

Liu Xiang 劉向 . *Lienu zhuan* 列女傳 [Biographies of Women], written in the Former Han dynasty, in 30 B.C. Reprint of Ming dynasty edition illustrated by Chou Shizhou 仇十洲 . Taipei: Guangwen shuju 廣文書局 , 1978.

Lu Xun. "My Views on Chastity." In *Silent China, Selected Writings of Lu Xun*, edited and translated by Gladys Yang. London: Oxford University Press, 1973.

Ren Darong 任達榮 , et al. *Zhongguo funu shilun ji* 中國婦女史論集 [Annotations on the History of Chinese Women], edited by Bao Jialin 鮑家麟 . Taipei: Mutong chubanshe 牧童出版社 , 1979.

Wang Fanting 王藩庭 . *Zhonghua lidai funu* 中華歷代婦女 [Women in Chinese History]. Taipei: Shangwu yinshuguan 商務印書館 , 1966.

Wu Ching-Tzu. *The Scholars* [Ju Lin Wai Shih, 儒林外史], translated by Yang Hsien-yi and Gladys Yang, illustrated by Chang Shih-Fa. Beijing: Foreign Languages Press, 1957.

Xie Jinqing 謝晉青. *Shijing zhi nuxing yanjiu* 詩經之女性研究 [Study of Women in the Odes]. Shanghai: Shangwu yinshuguan 商務印書館 , 1923.

Yumiko 申美子 . *Zhongguo tangdai funu yanjiu* 中國唐代婦女研究 [Research on Women of the Tang Dynasty]. Xeroxed. N.p, n.d. In University of Michigan Asia Library collection.

Zhao Cong 趙聰 . *Shijing lidi liange* 詩經裏的戀歌 [Love Songs in the Odes]. Hong Kong: Youlian tushu gongsi 友聯圖書公司 , 1964.

V. Divination

Feng Yingjing 馮應京 , comp. and ed. *Yueling guangyi* 月令廣義 [Clarification on "Yueling"], 8 vols. Annotated by Dai Renzeng 戴任增 . N.p.: Chen Bangtai 陳邦泰 , 1601.

Gao Daguan 高達觀 and Liu Zuguang 劉祖光, eds. *Jiazu* 家族 [Clan System]. Beida zhongguo minsu xuehui minsu congshu 北大中國民俗學會民俗叢書 [Research by University of Beijing Folklore Society Study Association], Set 7, Vol. 124. Beijing: Shilin dongfang wenhua shuju 士林東方文化書局 , 1973.

Gan Bao 干寶, ed. *Huitu sanjiao yuanliu soushen daquan* 繪圖三教源

流搜神大全 [Source of the Three Religions Complete with Appendix on Search for the Gods]. Illustrated. Taipei: Lianjing chuban shiye gongsi 聯經出版事業公司, 1980.

Tao Qian 陶潛, ed. *Soushen houji* 搜神後記 (More Search for the Gods) Beijing: Zhonghua shuju 中華書局, 1981.

Yan Bing 燕冰. *Zhongguo shenhua zazhi* 中國神話雜誌 [Chinese Mythology Magazine]. Beida zhongguo minsu xuehui minsu congshu 北大中國民俗學會民俗叢書 [Research by University of Beijing Folklore Society Study Association], 91. Beijing: Shilin dongfang wenhua shuju 士林東方文化書局, 1973.

Yuan Ke 袁珂. *Zhongguo gudai shenhua* 中國古代神話 [Old Legends from China]. Shanghai: Shangwu yinshuguan 商務印書館, 1950.

Zhang Xunqi 張迅齊. *Shenxian liezhuan* 神仙列傳 [Biographies of the Gods]. Taipei: Changchunshu shufang 常春樹書坊, 1973.

Zheng Zhenduo 鄭振鐸, ed. *Tianli lingqian* 天笠靈籤 (Temple Tallies from Tianli). Shanghai: Gudian wenxue chubanshe 古典文學出版社, 1950.

———. *Zhongguo suwenxue shi* 中國俗文學史 (History of Chinese Folklore). Beijing: Wenxue guji kanxing chuban 文學古籍刊行出版, 1959.

VI. Geography

Cressey, George B. *Asia's Lands and Peoples*. New York: McGraw Hill, 1944.

Daqing yitong yudi xinzhi 大清一統輿地新誌 [Supreme New Atlas of the Qing Dynasty], Vols. 1–12. Shanghai: Sanyang jingqiao tongwenguan shuju 三洋經橋同文館書局, 1902.

Fang Xu 方敘. *Danyang xianzhi* 丹陽縣志 [County Records of Danyang]. Revised and amended. Taipei: Huaxin yinshuguan 華新印書館, 1961.

Jintan xianzhi 金壇縣志 [County Records of Jintan], 2 vols. Revised,

1921. Taipei: County Association of Jintan in Taipei, lithographed by Jinshi yinzhi youxian gongsi 金氏印製有限公司, 1971.

Li Changpu 李長溥. *Fensheng dizhi: Jiangsu* 分省地志：江蘇 [Records of the Provinces: Jiangsu]. Shanghai: Zhonghua shuju 中華書局, 1936.

Tuan Yifu. *China.* The World's Landscape, edited by F. N. Houston, Aldine, Atherton, Chicago, New York, 1972.

Wang Peitang 王培棠, ed. *Jiangsu sheng xiangtu zhi* 江蘇省鄉土誌 [Records of the Countryside of Jiangsu Province], Vol. 1. Shanghai: Shanghai zhengfu yinxing 上海政府印行, 1937.

Yang Qi 楊棨, ed. *Zhongguo fangzhi congshu: Huazhong difang* 中國方志叢書：華中地方 [Topographies of China Series: Central China], Vol. 6, Nos. 1 and 2, *Jiangsu sheng jingkou shanshui zhi* 江蘇省京口山水志. Reprint of 1844 edition. Taipei: Chengwen chubanshe 成文出版社, 1970.

Zhonghua youzheng yutu 中華郵政輿圖 [Maps for the Chinese Postal Service]. Shanghai: Jiaotongbu youzheng zongju yinxing 交通部郵政總局印行, 1933.

Zhu Kebao 諸可寶, ed. *Zhongguo fangzhi congshu: Huazhong difang* 中國方志叢書：華中地方 [Topographies of China Series: Central China], No. 144, *Jiangsu quan sheng yutu* 江蘇全省輿圖 [Maps of Jiangsu Province]. Reprint of 1844 edition. Taipei: Chengwen chubanshe 成文出版社, 1974.

VII. Publication

Gao Shi 高士. "Boming nu shiren, He Shuangqing" 薄命女詩人一賀雙卿 [The Ill-fated Poet, He Shuangqing]. *Tiansheng bao* 天聲報, San Francisco, 19 September 1978.

Index on the Shuangqing's Poetry

A

B

C

G

H

I

J

K

L

T

V

W

X

Y

Subject Index

C

E

F

H

K

L

T

W

Z

Academic Monographs on Chinese Literature

Classical Chinese Literature: An Anthology of Translation, Volume 1: From Antiquity to the Tang Dynasty
Edited by John Minford and Joseph S. M. Lau (2000)

The Discourse on Foxes and Ghosts: Ji Yun and Eighteenth-Century Literati Storytelling
Leo Tak-hung Chan (1998)

The Vision of China in the English Literature of the Seventeenth and Eighteenth Centuries
Adrian Hsia (1998)

Ch'en Tzu-ang: Innovator in T'ang Dynasty
Richard M. W. Ho (1993)

Classical, Modern and Humane: Essays in Chinese Literature
Edited by John Minford and Siu-kit Wong (1989)

From Ritual to Allegory: Seven Essays in Early Chinese Poetry
C. H. Wang (1988)

Notes on Poetry from the Ginger Studio
Siu-kit Wong (1987)

The Literary Mind and the Carving of Dragons
Translated and annotated by Vincent Yu-chung Shih (1982)

甘露港
京口
黄山
小九華山
長山
五州山
萬頃洋
顧龍山
金壇縣城
天荒蕩
白龍蕩
錢資蕩
長蕩湖
茅山